The Nutcracker Ballet

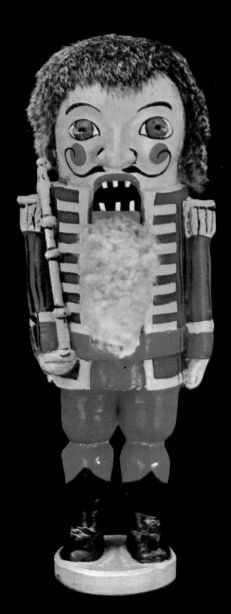

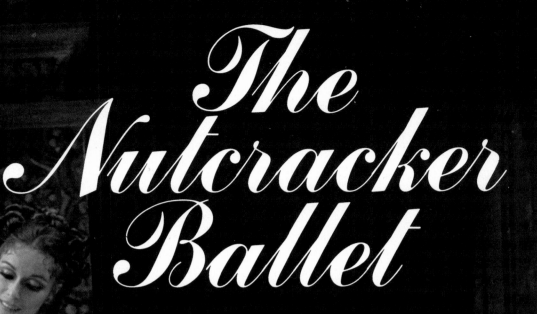

The Nutcracker Ballet

JACK ANDERSON

MAYFLOWER BOOKS
NEW YORK

A BISON BOOK

Author Jack Anderson
Editor Susan Garratt
Designer John Fitzmaurice

ISBN: 0 8317 6486 4
Produced by Bison Books Limited
Manufactured in Hong Kong
First American Edition

Half title page
The nutcracker doll.
Title page
Clara with her sister
Louise and Drossel-
meyer's nephew Karl on
Christmas Eve (London
Festival Ballet).
Contents page
Manola Asensio as the
Snow Queen with
Artistes of London
Festival Ballet in the
Snowflake Scene of
Act I.

A Holiday Tradition

Throughout the world a ballet is becoming as much a part of the Christmas tradition as the filled stocking, festive dinner, or decorated tree. The ballet is Peter Ilyitch Tchaikovsky's *The Nutcracker*. Come December companies everywhere stage it, and in many families attending a performance of *The Nutcracker* is a scrupulously observed holiday ritual. Christmas would not be Christmas without it.

The Nutcracker is in the repertoire of major companies which give splendidly decorated productions in great theaters and opera houses with symphony orchestras in the pit. *The Nutcracker* is also produced in small towns by local dancing schools. In these productions the school's pupils play children's roles, while their parents are often recruited for some of the adult parts or to swell the cast by serving as extras. Such productions are apt to be modest, with scenery and costumes made by volunteers. No matter how lavish or simple a production may be, if it is sincerely conceived and sincerely performed, *The Nutcracker* seldom fails, for *The Nutcracker* possesses the magic power to make people happy at Christmas.

It is a ballet about magic, about happiness and about Christmas. Versions differ, yet most tell essentially the same story, a story

Manelle Jaye as Clara and Terry Hayworth as Drosselmeyer in a London Festival Ballet production.

which goes something like this: 'Once upon a time. . . .' That is the way, of course, fairy tales usually begin. But since *The Nutcracker* is a balletic fairy tale, it cannot say 'once upon a time' with words. Instead there is an overture, quiet delicate music to calm audiences and make them wonder what will happen next. Now the curtain rises.

The scene is a comfortable middle-class parlor of a house in a German town a hundred years ago. Dr. Stahlbaum, a member of the town council, is giving a Christmas Eve party and all the members of his family are excited, particularly his children, Clara and Fritz (in some productions they have other names, but Clara and Fritz are common names for these characters). Clara is a slightly shy, dreamy little girl. Fritz, however, is a real scamp. Sometimes they quarrel and their parents have to step in as mediators. Nevertheless they are fond of each other and tonight they are united in their admiration of the Christmas tree which fills one corner of the parlor.

Guests arrive. Among the grownups are uncles and aunts. Some who live a great distance away only see each other at Christmas, so this is a time for handshakes and hugs. Grandfather and grandmother come to the party, too. The frosty night air has made their joints ache and, slightly shaky on their feet, they have to sit down and rest awhile when they enter the parlor. A glass of sherry soon warms them up. The cousins and the friends of Clara and Fritz arrive.

Gifts are exchanged and candies are passed around. The children play with their new toys. Although the little girls try to behave, the boys get rowdy and have to be hushed by their elders.

All this is a perfectly ordinary nineteenth-century Christmas party. There seems nothing magical about it, yet *The Nutcracker* is a ballet about magic. A strange thing about magic, though, is that it occurs under what might otherwise seem the most ordinary everyday circumstances. That is one reason why magic takes people by surprise.

And here now is the first hint of magic: another guest arrives, a latecomer. This is Drosselmeyer, Clara's godfather, and a very odd guest he is. An elderly gentleman, he dresses in a somber old-fashioned style. He has only one good eye and wears a black patch over the bad one. Though bony and slightly stooped, he commands attention. His fingers are as agile as a magician's fingers and he can perform conjuring tricks. He is also a clockmaker and an inventor who knows how to fashion all sorts of mechanical marvels. He has brought some to the party: life-sized dolls which, when they are wound up, jump and dance and whirl about until their mechanism runs down. Everyone is fond of Drosselmeyer, but there is something decidedly mysterious about him. With Drosselmeyer this year is his nephew, a boy of Clara's age or perhaps just a bit older. Clara has never met him before, and when they are introduced she decides she likes him very much. He has the glamour of being a

stranger. He is also charming and courteous, with manners almost like those of a grownup.

More gifts are exchanged. Drosselmeyer gives Clara a strange present: a nutcracker shaped like a little man with a long nose and a big mouth who cracks nuts with his teeth. Although it is a grotesque toy, Clara grows fond of her gnomelike nutcracker and happily demonstrates its nutcracking abilities for her friends. When Fritz sees it, he decides he wants it for himself. Pulling it away from Clara, he breaks the nutcracker's jaw in the scuffle. Clara is heartbroken, but Drosselmeyer fixes the toy and dries her tears.

One last dance brings the party to an end. The guests depart and the Stahlbaum children are sent off to bed. Clara cannot sleep, however, and she tiptoes downstairs for a peek at her nutcracker. Clasping it in her arms, she curls up on the sofa and dozes off.

Her mother, Frau Stahlbaum, walks through the rooms of the house, making sure that everything is in order after the party. When she sees her daughter asleep on the sofa, her first impulse is to wake her. No,

Left
Illustration of Dr Drosselmeyer by Bertall from the 1847 version of Alexandre Dumas' retelling of Hoffmann's *The Nutcracker and the King of Mice.*
Above right
Clara is delighted with the nutcracker her godfather has just presented to her. This production by the Cincinnati Ballet Company was first staged in 1974 and was set in nineteenth-century Cincinnati.
Below
Scene in the Stahlbaum's parlor from the 1937 Vic-Wells Theatre production designed by Mstislav Doboujinsky.

she decides, let the child sleep here in the shadow of the Christmas tree, her toys and presents scattered about her. So she simply covers Clara with a shawl to prevent her from being chilled. Clara sleeps on.

Then something—perhaps the sound of her mother's departing footsteps, perhaps some other, unexplained sound—causes her to stir. She rubs her eyes. How strange the parlor looks at night in the dark. Sinister shadows cross the floor, shadows as black as Drosselmeyer's winter cloak. Clara even imagines she sees Drosselmeyer still lurking in the room—in that corner, for instance. No, in that corner over there.

Clara hears peculiar things as well—rustlings, scurryings. The noises intensify and the room brightens with a curious glow. The candles have relighted themselves on the Christmas tree, and the tree itself is growing bigger. Up and up it rises until the star at its tip pokes through the ceiling. Now all the children's toys—the dolls, brother Fritz's wooden soldiers, Clara's beloved nutcracker—come magically alive. How wonderful this is, thinks Clara.

Below
Illustration by Bertall of the little girl Mary comforting her broken nutcracker.

But there is also black magic at work. Suddenly the room is invaded by mice—ugly, nasty, horrid mice. They scurry hither and thither. They scamper about, flicking their tails and twitching their noses. They have come to rob and plunder. They gobble every piece of candy they can find. Led by their fearsome king—the biggest, fattest mouse of all—they start to attack the dolls. The dolls retaliate, and under the command of the Nutcracker, an army of wooden soldiers marches against the mice. Valiant though the soldiers are, the mice possess brute force and manage to nip or knock over all the toys.

Only the Nutcracker is left unharmed, and he is engaged in a duel with the Mouse King. Swords flash. Clara watches with baited breath. The Nutcracker is an agile swordsman, yet the Mouse King seems to be winning. Wanting to help the Nutcracker, Clara takes off one of her slippers and throws it at the Mouse King. The blow angers him and he glances back as though to squeak, 'Who dared to do that?' Distracted by the slipper, he takes his attention away from the duel for an instant—a fatal instant, for while his head is turned the Nutcracker manages to give the Mouse King a mortal wound. Their

sovereign dead, the rest of the mice skitter back into their holes. The toys are saved.

The Nutcracker thanks Clara for her kindness. Now comes the greatest magic of all. He is no longer a nutcracker, and no longer a toy. He is transformed into a handsome young man: into Drosselmeyer's nephew, to be exact, and he promises to take Clara to an enchanted realm. The walls of the Stahlbaum house vanish. Clara and young Drosselmeyer find themselves in a forest of snow-covered fir trees. Snow starts falling, the snowflakes turning into dancing snow fairies. As the children pass through the forest, the first act of *The Nutcracker* comes to an end.

In the second, and last, act young Drosselmeyer keeps his promise to Clara. The setting is a palace in the Land of Sweets, a

kingdom ruled by the Sugarplum Fairy. This benign monarch greets the children and asks how they happened to come her way. Young Drosselmeyer tells their story—not with words (for this is a ballet), but in an old gestural language called mime which enables him to recount all the marvelous adventures of Christmas Eve. Impressed with the children's bravery, the Sugarplum Fairy rewards them with a grand entertainment.

Dancers representing good things to eat and drink such as tea, coffee, hot chocolate, and candy canes come from far places—from Spain, China, and Arabia, for example—just to perform for Clara and her friend. A garden of flowers waltzes for them. Most impressive of all is a dance for the Sugarplum Fairy and her Prince, a kind of dance the seasoned balletgoer terms a *pas de deux*.

Left
The Nutcracker in battle in Act I of the American Ballet Theater production.
Below
The children play with their Christmas toys in the Royal Ballet production premiered in 1968 and designed by Nicholas Georgiadis.

All parties, however—even magic ones— come to an end, and finally the Sugarplum Fairy tells Clara it is time to go home. In the wink of an eye, home she is, back on the parlor sofa. It has all been a dream. Or has it?

So goes the usual story of *The Nutcracker*. It is customary to call it a children's story and to regard the ballet as a children's show. But sophisticated adults have been known to get misty-eyed at *Nutcracker* performances. Moreover to be childlike is not the same as to be childish. For all its apparent artlessness *The Nutcracker* may be far from simple. Like that other children's classic, Lewis Carroll's *Alice in Wonderland*, Tchaikovsky's ballet has attracted serious attention. Critics have scrutinized it for hidden meanings, psychologists have psychoanalyzed it, and poets have rhapsodized over it.

The history of *The Nutcracker*'s productions is almost as curious as the ballet's own fairy-tale plot. At first Tchaikovsky felt disinclined to compose the music. The choreographer who was originally supposed to devise the dances fell ill and had to entrust the project to an assistant, and the St Petersburg premiere in 1892 was, at best, only moderately successful. When some critics called the story silly, Tchaikovsky sank into a depression. Even while the ballet was new dancers and other choreographers began to introduce changes into it, so many changes that most of the original choreography has been lost. Nevertheless *The Nutcracker* kept being staged and today there are scores of productions. People never tire of it and the ballet's popularity shows no signs of diminishing. Most productions follow the familiar scenario. However, some do not, while still others attempt to give that scenario a novel twist. There have been Freudian *Nutcracker*s, acrobatic *Nutcracker*s, *Nutcracker*s set in countries other than Germany, *Nutcracker*s without mice, and *Nutcracker*s without a Sugarplum Fairy. There have even been a few *Nutcracker*s which have had nothing to do with Christmas. Yet *The Nutcracker* has managed to survive—and to thrive as a hardy toy, and one not for children only.

The First Nutcracker

The Nutcracker came about as an attempt to provide one balletic success with an equally successful sequel. In 1890 the ballet company of the Maryinsky Theater in St Petersburg had staged *The Sleeping Beauty*. Although, at first, its music bewildered some audiences because of its symphonic richness, it soon became apparent that this production was one of the triumphs of Russian ballet. It was such a success that a year later, in 1891, Ivan Alexandrovitch Vsevolojsky, Director of the Imperial Theaters in St Petersburg, proposed to reunite the creators of *The Sleeping Beauty*: Tchaikovsky, the composer, and Marius Petipa, the choreographer. If

they could work together on a new fairy-tale ballet, he thought, perhaps the result would be another triumph.

Russians were proud of their ballet—and with justice, since by the late nineteenth century Russian ballet was the strongest in the world, particularly the Maryinsky Ballet of St Petersburg. In other countries ballet was declining. Paris, which had been the center of balletic innovation since the seventeenth century, had entered upon an era of choreographic triviality. London, Vienna, and New York had also known moments of glory, but ballet was fading in those cities, too, until by the end of the century ballet in

The party guests of the Royal Ballet waltz in the Stahlbaum's parlor.

many places was considered nothing more—and certainly nothing more profound—than a pretext for allowing shapely ladies to twirl about and show off their pretty legs.

That ballet thrived in St Petersburg was, in part, due to the Imperial patronage which had existed since 1766 when Catherine II established the Directorate of the Imperial Theaters, which had charge over drama, opera, and ballet. Russian theaters were truly state theaters, for the tsars personally appointed their directors, attended all major performances, and often awarded prizes at the graduation ceremonies of the ballet schools attached to the theaters. Members of the Royal family were also known, on occasion, to choose ballet dancers as their mistresses. Artistically St Petersburg ballet attained a high level because of the existence of the Maryinsky's ballet school which insured the perpetuation of the best classical tradition, producing generation after generation of superbly trained dancers. These dancers, in turn, had opportunities to work in the theater with distinguished choreographers and ballet masters, both Russian and foreign.

Right
Marius Petipa in 1869. He planned the scenario for *The Nutcracker* but a serious illness forced him to turn the choreography over to Lev Ivanov, his assistant.
Below left
Carlotta Grisi and Lucien Petipa, brother of Marius, in the farewell performance of *The Peri* at Drury-Lane in 1843. Marius Petipa was from a family of dancers.
Below
Mademoiselle Plunkett and Lucien Petipa in *Les Amazons* at Covent Garden Theatre in 1848.

Of these the most important was the French-born Marius Petipa (1818–1910). A member of a family of dancers, he toured Europe as a young man, and in 1847 accepted an offer to dance at the Maryinsky. He assumed that the appointment in distant Russia would be a short-term one and that in a few years he would be back in Paris. Instead he remained at the Maryinsky until his retirement in 1903. He began to choreograph, achieving his first success in 1862 with *The Daughter of the Pharaoh*, a ballet about Egypt. Following its production, he became increasingly important at the Maryinsky, eventually reigning as the virtual dictator of St Petersburg ballet. Oddly enough, despite his long stay in Russia, he never learned to speak fluent Russian, preferring to converse with his colleagues in French. They usually had little difficulty in understanding it since, at the time, French was prized in Russia as the language of culture and diplomacy.

Petipa had to be something of a diplomat, staging productions which would please the balletgoers of his day, who tended to be a special group of people. They included, of

course, the Royal family and the nobles. The theaters were also open to everyone—theoretically, at least. In actuality what tended to happen was that people bought subscription tickets for an entire season, renewing their subscriptions season after season. This made tickets difficult to obtain for the casual theatergoer and even for the theatrical devotee newly arrived in St Petersburg from some other city. Season subscriptions were considered so valuable that, after a subscriber died, his heirs would sometimes wrangle in court about who had legal rights to his seat. Among the members of the regular audience in St Petersburg were fanatic lovers of ballet who were nicknamed the balletomanes. They religiously attended every ballet evening, knew in detail all the ballets in the repertoire, and argued endlessly over the strengths and weaknesses of each of the company's dancers. A knowledgeable lot, they also tended to be conservative, distrusting innovation. Consequently they often exerted a retardative influence. In choreographing his ballets, Petipa had to balance his own standards of artistry (including, occasionally, a desire to innovate) with the necessity of pleasing an

Below
Tchaikovsky among his relatives.

audience which, if cultivated, did not always countenance departures from established tradition. His success is reflected in the very length of his tenure at the Maryinsky.

In 1881 Petipa gained an important ally when Vsevolojsky was appointed Director of the St Petersburg theaters, remaining in charge until 1899. Despite the importance of the post—which involved overseeing all theatrical activities in the city—it did not invariably go to truly qualified men. Bestowed as a favor by the tsar, it was sometimes regarded as a sinecure by its occupant, who would collect a comfortable salary and never bother to allocate money to stage new productions or refurbish old ones. Unlike some of his predecessors, Vsevolojsky (1835–1909) possessed a genuine love of music and ballet and helped inspire what Petipa termed 'a real blossoming forth of the arts in the St Petersburg theaters.' A rich, educated dilettante and something of a dandy, Vsevolojsky had served with the Russian Embassy in Paris before receiving his theatrical appointment. Petipa admired him as 'a true courtier' and dedicated his memoirs to him.

Vsevolojsky wanted his St Petersburg productions to be harmonious collaborations between distinguished composers, dancers, and designers working together to reach a common goal. A painter himself (a second-rate one, however), Vsevolojsky often designed Maryinsky productions, including the costumes for 25 ballets. Although critics occasionally chided his designs for being too florid, they did attest to

Below
The Tchaikovsky house-museum in the town of Votkinsk in Russia.

E.T.A. HOFFMANN

his desire to make Maryinsky stagings artistically unified. These attempts to achieve distinction in all aspects of theatrical production make Vsevolojsky a forerunner of Serge Diaghilev, who as impresario and ballet director revolutionized dance at the beginning of the twentieth century by commissioning works from leading choreographers, composers, and painters. Vsevolojsky was never as radical in his tastes as Diaghilev, but he did much to raise standards at the Maryinsky.

He was especially concerned about that theater's musical standards. Since 1871 the Viennese-born Ludwig Minkus had served as the Maryinsky's official composer of ballet music. Minkus' ballet music was rhythmically rousing with lilting tunes. It was eminently danceable, and Minkus could compose in a hurry. Unfortunately, though it usually had charm, this music was seldom distinguished and almost never profound. Yet, because he was the theater's official ballet composer, he had to be considered the first choice of composer whenever a choreographer wished to create a new ballet. As long as Minkus was still at the Maryinsky and still composing, there was little chance of drastically upgrading the quality of the theater's music. Vsevolojsky found a way out of this dilemma by securing a pension for Minkus in 1886. Then he left the post of official ballet composer vacant, which gave him the freedom to commission scores from any composer he wished.

One composer he particularly wished would write for the ballet was Peter Ilyitch Tchaikovsky (1840–1893). Vsevolojsky admired Tchaikovsky and in 1888 persuaded Tsar Nicholas III to bestow a life annuity of 3000 rubles upon the composer. Before encountering Vsevolojsky, Tchaikovsky had had only one experience in working on a ballet production. He had composed *Swan Lake* in 1877 for Moscow's Bolshoi Ballet. It had not been a success and Tchaikovsky did not essay the genre again until Vsevolojsky and Petipa commissioned *The Sleeping Beauty*. Obtaining ballet music from Tchaikovsky was a major acquisition, just as it would be another major acquisition when Vsevolojsky and Petipa persuaded Alexander Glazunov to compose *Raymonda* in 1898.

Petipa and Vsevolojsky got on well together. Both were francophile in taste and both loved spectacular productions. Their *Sleeping Beauty* had been a spectacle on the grandest scale based upon the French fairy tales of Charles Perrault. Their new ballet would also be a fairy-tale spectacle, but this time its basic literary source was German (although it came to their attention via France). Vsevolojsky devised a senario based upon E T A Hoffmann's long short story, *The Nutcracker and the King of the Mice*. To this day Hoffmann (1776–1822) is regarded as one of the greatest of all fantasy writers, and he was enormously popular during the nineteenth century, his influence extending beyond literature into opera and dance. His works have inspired several operas, the most familiar of them being Offenbach's *Tales of Hoffmann*, which derives from three of his stories. Among the ballets which, like *The Nutcracker*, come from Hoffmann is *Coppélia*, produced by the Paris Opéra Ballet in 1870 with music by Léo Delibes and choreography by Arthur Saint-Léon. In a sense *The Nutcracker* and *Coppélia* are dilutions of Hoffmann; both are essentially lighthearted, but Hoffmann's stories often contain a strong element of the grotesque, sinister, or even the demonic.

Born in Prussia, Hoffmann studied law and held posts in the municipal bureaucracies of several cities. However, the arts were his real passions—particularly music, which he so adored that in honor of Wolfgang Amadeus Mozart he changed one of his middle names from Wilhelm to Amadeus. He founded an orchestra in Warsaw, served as musical director for theaters in Bamberg, Dresden, and Leipzig, composed two symphonies and ten operas, and wrote trenchant music criticism under the pseudonym of Johannes Kreisler which supported the new Romantic trends in music, including the compositions of Beethoven. After music, his great love was writing. Hoffmann wrote in the genre known as the *Kunstmärchen*, the art fairy tale as distinct from the folk tale. This form was popular among the Romantics, since it encouraged flights of fancy and excursions into the grotesque.

To his neighbors Hoffmann must have appeared as curious as any character out of his tales. A small, dark, wiry man with deep-set eyes and bushy hair, he was ever restless, ever plagued by nervous tics. His hands and feet twitched constantly, as did the features of his face. His conversation was as restless as his person. Epigrams, jokes, puns, serious pronouncements, and imaginative speculations poured out of him without pause, especially after a drink or two. Hoffmann also fell into fits of melancholy, which only alcohol could cure. He drank heavily and even sold the rights to his first book for a cellar of wine. Eventually alcohol and exhaustion took their toll. Hoffmann contracted digestive difficulties, a degeneration of the liver, and a mysterious neural ailment

Right
Vivien Cockburn and John Hiatt in the Snow Scene *pas de deux* for Ballet West.
Right inset
The title page of the musical score to *The Nutcracker* ballet.
Below
Illustration of Drosselmeyer by Bertall.

which led to a gradual paralysis of his body, beginning with the feet. For this condition his doctor prescribed a remedy as terrible as the disease: the placing of red-hot pokers against the base of the spine. Despite his spells of melancholy, Hoffmann tried to preserve an optimistic view of things and on his deathbed, although paralyzed and unable to write, he continued to dictate stories, the last of them called ironically enough, *The Recovery*.

The Nutcracker and the King of the Mice, written in 1816, was first published in a children's collection, *Kindermärchen*, along with other stories by C W Contessa and Friedrich Baron de la Motte Fouqué. Hoffmann did not regard the piece as being entirely successful. Nevertheless it achieved popularity, not only in German-speaking countries, but beyond their borders, due to a French adaptation by Alexandre Dumas *père* called *The Nutcracker of Nuremberg*. It was this version which Vsevolojsky and Petipa knew. There are slight differences between the versions, but the basic plot is the same:

At a Christmas party in Nuremberg, a city famous for its toymakers, a little girl is given a nutcracker by her eccentric godfather, Drosselmeyer. Hoffmann says he is short; Dumas says he is tall. Both writers are agreed that he is wrinkled and round-shouldered, wears a black patch over one eye, has a wig made of white glass, and spends his free time fixing clocks and constructing mechanical toys. The little girl's nutcracker is accidentally broken by her brother, and after the party, she remains to bid the toy invalid goodnight. Suddenly the parlor is invaded by mice. Toy soldiers, led by the wounded Nutcracker, make a gallant defense, but they are outnumbered. At the height of the battle, the Nutcracker, like another desperate warrior before him, cries out, 'A horse, a horse, my kingdom for a horse!' Just as the mice seem ready to triumph, the little girl throws her slipper at them and they retreat.

American Ballet Theater
party scene.

This is the story we know from the ballet. The next day, however, Drosselmeyer tells his godchild another story, a story the ballet never tells us. Here is the story Drosselmeyer tells in these literary versions.

There once was a princess named Pirlipat. Because her parents had quarrelled with mice, the mice swore revenge upon her. Therefore Pirlipat's bed was watched every night by guardians, very much like the guardian angels in *Hansel and Gretel*, except that each of these guardians held a big, purring cat. Alas, one night all the cats and all the guardians fell asleep at the same time, and the Mouse Queen turned the princess into a dwarf.

A wise clockmaker (named, by a strange coincidence, Drosselmeyer) discovered that Pirlipat would be restored to her natural beauty if a young man cracked the Krakatuk nut. This was easier said than done, for not even a cannon could penetrate its hard thick shell. Nonetheless Drosselmeyer found a young man who could do it. By another strange coincidence, it was his own nephew. (Here, says Dumas, is the origin of the old saying, 'That's a hard nut to crack.')

Just as everybody was planning to live happily ever after, nephew Drosselmeyer accidentally stepped on the Mouse Queen's tail and was himself transformed into a dwarf. This spell could be broken only if he slew the Mouse Queen's son and heir, the seven-headed Mouse King.

When the little girl heard this, she was convinced that her Nutcracker was really the bewitched nephew Drosselmeyer. She supplied him with a sword borrowed from a tin soldier, the Mouse King was slain and she and nephew Drosselmeyer sailed off to Confectionary Castle in a seashell drawn by dolphins. Then she woke up and found herself at home in bed.

Time passed. Several Christmases later, Drosselmeyer introduced her to his real nephew, a handsome fellow who was able to perform the curious parlor trick of cracking nuts with his front teeth. The girl was sure this was her childhood Nutcracker Prince.

They were married, and again went off to a candy kingdom. There they are still living today.

As the basis for a ballet scenario, Hoffmann's original tale is less than ideal. With its tale within a tale, with its digressions and multiple transformations, it is much too long and unwieldy. Vsevolojsky therefore simplified it to produce the scenario familiar to us today, smoothing out the story and softening its grotesquerie. Hoffmann can be almost lurid at times; for example, when describing the little girl's encounter with the seven-headed Mouse King, he speaks of how 'the horrible Mouse King came and sat on her shoulder, foamed a blood-red foam out of all his seven mouths, and chattering and grinding his teeth, he hissed. . . .' Dumas toned down some of Hoffmann's wilder extravagances, yet he, too, offers pungent descriptive passages, as when he says that Drosselmeyer's face 'was as wrinkled as an apple that has withered and fallen from the tree.' Similarly Vsevolojsky softened some of the ambiguously erotic emotions felt by Hoffmann's seven-year-old heroine. Balletgoers who have read Hoffmann may also be surprised at a number of minor discrepancies between the story and the ballet: for instance, the little girl, so often called Clara in the ballet, is Marie in the story, Clara being the name of one of her dolls.

By taking the wrinkles out of Hoffmann and Dumas, Vsevolojsky fashioned a straightforward balletic plot which would satisfy the current love for spectacle. If anything, he may have made the story too bland —a charge brought against *The Nutcracker* to this day. Vsevolojsky presented his scenario to Tchaikovsky and Petipa. To Tchaikovsky he also offered another commission: the commission to write a short opera which could be premiered along with *The Nutcracker* on the same program. Out of this request came the opera *Iolanta*.

The scenario for *The Nutcracker* disappointed Tchaikovsky once he had perused it. He considered the theme distinctly inferior to *The Sleeping Beauty* and began work

Above
Illustration by Bertall of the little girl who is called Mary in the adaptation of the Nutcracker story by Dumas.

Right
Bonnie Wyckoff as the twelve-year-old Maria in the Royal Winnipeg Ballet production staged by John Neumeier. In this production the setting was changed to a birthday party.

Москва. 15 Іюля 1877 г.

№ 25

letters and Madame von Meck gave Tchaikovsky moral support during his recurrent periods of depression. She gave him financial support, too, in the form of an annuity. This peculiar arrangement—a Platonic affair carried on entirely by correspondence—came abruptly to an end in December 1890 when Madame von Meck told Tchaikovsky that she was on the brink of ruin and could no longer assist him. Thereafter all letters ceased and Tchaikovsky was left desolate.

One wonders what sort of score Tchaikovsky might have written if Vsevolojsky's ballet scenario had preserved some of Hoffmann's darker tones, for the urbane, cultivated composer was, like Hoffmann, prone to melancholy. The second of five children, he was a frail, sensitive boy. Although he had music lessons as a child, his father thought it better for him to be a lawyer and so, like Hoffmann, he attended law school, graduating in 1859. He became a clerk in the Ministry of Justice, a job he hated but which provided him with steady work. He started composing music to amuse himself. Then, at the age of 23, he decided to devote his life to music and enrolled at the St Petersburg Conservatory.

If the decision to become a composer allowed Tchaikovsky the freedom to do what he most wanted to do, it also increased his insecurity. He could no longer count upon a regular income, nor could he know in advance whether he would be a success or a dismal failure as a musician. His self-doubts increased and he soon suffered the first of several nervous breakdowns, falling prey to

Above
A page from a letter to Madame von Meck from Tchaikovsky dated 15 July 1877.
Left
The Tchaikovsky house-museum in the town of Votkinsk in Udmurtia, Russia.

on the score in January 1891 without enthusiasm. He wrote to his brother Modeste, 'The subject of *Casse-Noisette* [*Nutcracker's* French title] pleases me very little. I am very tired and in reality suffer a great deal. Is it wise to accept the offer of the Imperial Theaters? My brain is empty.' But there were reasons having nothing to do with music which may have induced his mental disquiet. For 13 years—ever since 1876 when she commissioned a short piece from him—Tchaikovsky had corresponded with a well-to-do woman, Nadezhda von Meck. During all that time, they never once met. They exchanged frank

Above
Tchaikovsky's grand piano in the house-museum at Klin.
Left
The nutcracker doll which Drosselmeyer presents to Clara, his goddaughter, at the Christmas party.
Above right
View from the garden of Tchaikovsky's house at Klin.
Right
Tchaikovsky's desk at Klin.

the most irrational fears and obsessions. Thus, conducting an orchestra terrified him because he was sure that someday, while he was at the podium his head would literally fall off his neck. His personal life was equally unhappy. A homosexual, Tchaikovsky also accepted the social mores of his period which condemned his sexual orientation. In 1877 he married Antonina Milukova, but the marriage soon failed and he attempted suicide.

His death in 1893 during a cholera epidemic has raised questions which have never been fully answered. One night he awoke from sleep feeling thirsty and ill, and to slake his thirst he drank a glass of tap water without first boiling it as a precaution against infection. Whether this was purely an oversight or whether Tchaikovsky was deliberately flirting with death, no one can say. Tchaikovsky did contract the disease, however, and died several days later.

Tchaikovsky used music to exorcise his private demons and was most happy when he was composing. He set to work on *Iolanta* and *The Nutcracker* and discovered as he proceeded that his initial indifference to *The Nutcracker* was turning to active interest. Composing music for Petipa was not simply a matter of the composer's whim. Petipa was a meticulous workman who liked to plan in advance as many details of a ballet as possible. At home he would devise poses and groupings by moving little figures like chessmen about on a tabletop. He made notes to himself and would sometimes start work on choreography before the music had been delivered to him. When the score arrived, he would study it carefully, sometimes revising his choreography to fit the music, sometimes sending the score back for musical revisions.

Petipa was able to start choreographing a scene without music because even before the music was completed he had some idea of what it would be like. Whenever a composer agreed to write a score for him, Petipa sent that composer an outline of the action with detailed instructions about what sort of music he wished, measure by measure. Many composers might have chafed to work within such severe restrictions; Tchaikovsky, apparently, did not. If anything he thrived on

them. He had written *The Sleeping Beauty* in accordance with Petipa's specifications, and the resultant score was a masterpiece of its kind. Now he was writing *The Nutcracker* under similar conditions. As an example of how strict Petipa could be in his demands upon composers, here are his specifications for *The Nutcracker*:

At the rise of the curtain, the large dining room is lit by only one candelabra.

1 The President and his wife and guests decorate the tree.
   (Delicate, mysterious music 64 bars.)
   9 o'clock strikes; at each chime of the clock, the owl on the top of it flaps its wings. Everything is ready and it is time to call the children.
   (All this takes place during the 64 bars.)

2 The fir tree is burning brightly, as if with magic.
   (Modulated music 8 bars.)

3 The door is thrown open.
   (Noisy and happy music for the children's entrance, 24 bars.)

4 The children stop, full of amazement and delight.
   (A few bars for the children. Tremolo.)

5 The President orders a march to be played.
   (March 64 bars.)
   Each child receives a present.
   All this takes place during the march.

6 *(Gallop for the children. 48 bars.)*

6b Entrance of the guests dressed very grandly.
   16 bars for entrance. Then a rococo dance. Tempo di Minuet. 'A good journey on the road to Du Mol.'

7 General amazement at the appearance of the Counsellor Drosselmeyer.
   (At his entrance the clock strikes, the owl appears to flap his wings. The music becomes, by degrees, a little more frightening and even comic. A broad movement from ·16 to 24 bars.)
   The children, frightened, hide their heads in their parents' dresses. They are pacified, seeing that he brings some toys. Here the character of the music changes gradually.
   (24 bars, the music becomes less dull, more clear and finally changes to joy.)

* Petipa's remark: 'I'll have to make up my mind, I prefer the characters of Harlequin and Columbine.'

8 The President's two children nervously await the presentation of Drosselmeyer's presents.
   (For this, No. 8, 8 bars of fairly grand music with pauses, in order for a cabbage to be shown and the same eight bars (repeated) for a pie, and the same pauses.)
   'Pas with baskets.' (Drosselmeyer orders them to bring in two baskets, from one he takes a large head of cabbage, this is Clara's present—from the other a large pie—this is for Fritz. Seeing such uninteresting presents, the children and their parents seem disappointed.)
   (For this movement, only 4 bars, with a chord of astonishment—everyone exchanges glances.)

9 Drosselmeyer, smiling, commands them to place the two presents before him—
   8 bars, motif of a mazurka.
   He winds them up—
   another 8 bars mazurka, during which the creakings of the key are heard.
   The children are overjoyed, out of the cabbage appears a large doll and from the pie a soldier.
   (Another ·16 bars mazurka for this little scene.)

10 *Pas de Deux.* (The clock is showing some time after 10 o'clock.)
   48 bars pizzicato with plucked strings of a good rhythmic valse.

11 Drosselmeyer orders them to bring in two large boxes from which appear the 'Diable and Diablesse.'* (Under these words is written 'Harlequin and Columbine.')
   16 bars, in order to give an opportunity for a change to another Pas.
   Demoniacal *Pas* of Dolls on elastic.
   (2/4 fairly quick and syncopated—48 bars.)

12 Clara and Fritz are now overjoyed, they thank Drosselmeyer and go to fetch the toys.
   (16 bars of a happy, graceful andantino.)
   The parents forbid them to play with such beautiful things.
   (The andantino becomes more serious. 8 bars.)
   Clara cries. Fritz is naughty. This occurs during the last 8 bars. In order to console them, the old Counsellor takes from his pocket a third present, the nutcracker; they can play with it as much as they like.
   (Another 8 bars of a more animated Andantino.)

13 Clara is immediately enraptured with the toy.

Now a polka tempo begins:

Clara asks the Counsellor what the present is for. In the music one hears 'Crack, crack' (under these words is written the 'knack, knack') all in the polka motif. Fritz, hearing the 'Knack, knack' of the toy, becomes interested, and, in his turn, wants to crack a nut. Clara does not want to give the toy to him. The parents tell Clara that the nutcracker does not belong to her alone. Clara gives her darling to her brother and sees with horror, that Fritz cracks two nuts with it. After this he pushes such a big nut into the nutcracker's mouth, that its teeth are broken—'Krack!' All this takes place during the 48 bars of the polka.

14 Fritz laughing, throws the nutcracker away—

8 bars of very animated music.

Clara picks it up and with caresses, tries to console her pet.

(Another 8 bars—less animated and more melodious.)

She takes her doll from its bed and puts the nutcracker in its place. This takes place during the 8 bars.

15 Lullaby.

16 bars for the Lullaby, which changes into a Fanfare of horns, trumpets and other brass instruments.

At this, Fritz and his friends tease Clara.

Another 16 bars of Lullaby, and again the same noise in the instruments—8 bars.

16 In order to stop this uproar, the President asks the guests to dance the 'Grossvater'.

(8 bars before the dance begins.)

17 'Grossvater.'

18 The guests thank the President and his wife and go out. The children are told to go to bed. Clara asks to be allowed to take the poor nutcracker with her. Her parents refuse. She goes out sorrowfully, after she has wrapped her pet up.

(Graceful march, finishing in a diminuendo. From 24 to 32 bars.)

19 An empty stage. The moon lights up the dining-room through the window.

(This phrase is underlined twice and under it Petipa has written 'NO'.)

(8 bars, mysterious and delicate music.)

Clara, in her nightdress, quickly returns to look at her darling pet once again.

(8 bars, even more mysterious for her entrance.)

Something frightens her—2 bars. She trembles, she goes up to the nutcracker's bed from where, it seems, a fantastic light is flickering.

8 bars of fantastic and still more mysterious music.

The clock strikes midnight.

Pause in the music.

Whilst the clock strikes midnight, she looks at the clock and sees with terror, that the owl has turned into Drosselmeyer, who looks at her with his sneering smile.

After her fright a tremolo of terror.

She wants to run away, but has not the strength. This occurs during the tremolo.

20 In the stillness of the night, she hears the mice scratching. She tries to gather strength to go away, but the mice appear on all sides.

Immediately after the tremolo—4 bars, during which are heard the scratching of the mice and another 4 bars for the squeakings.

Then—full of terror—she wants to take the poor nutcracker and run away, but her fear is too great. She sinks down in a chair. Everything disappears.

(After the squeaking of the mice, another 8 bars of accelerated movement, finished in a chord.)

Just as she sinks into a chair:

21 The back door opens and the fir tree seems to grow enormous.

(48 bars of fantastic music with a grandiose crescendo.)

22 The sentinel on guard cries out:—'Who goes there?' The mice do not answer.

2 bars for the cry and 2 bars for the silence.

The sentinel fires, *one or 2 bars.*

The dolls are frightened. *2 bars of fear.*

The sentinels will be like Hares—and are drummers—

8 bars to wake them up and 8 bars to beat the alarm, after this, 4 to 8 bars to form them into lines for battle.

The battle—48 bars—2/4.

The mice are victorious,

(this is after 48 bars and the battle 8 bars),

and eat up the gingerbread soldiers (sentinels). Let there be an opportunity of hearing how the mice gnaw the gingerbread.

23 The Mouse King appears and is welcomed by his warriors.

For his entrance gnawing, discontented music, grating on the ears, in which is heard 'couee, couee' (Hurrah). For the entrance of of the King, 8 bars and 4 bars for the Hurrah (Couee, Couee).

24 The Nutcracker calls to his old guards. He commands—'To arms.'

4 bars and 8 bars so that the troops can be set out in battle formation once again.

25 A second battle begins.

The 2/4 is continued.

A discharge of guns, the rattle of grapeshot, the firing and shrill cries are heard. *96 bars.*

26 In order to protect the Nutcracker, Clara throws her shoe at the Mouse King. (Petipa's remark:—'During the fight, the dolls come down off the fir tree and begin plucking off the cotton wool, and then Clara falls into a faint.')

2 bars for the shrill cry and 6 bars for the squeakings of the mice, who disappear. This happens at the end of the 96 bars.

27 The Nutcracker turns into a handsome Prince.

(1 or 2 chords.)

He rushes to assist Clara, who comes to herself.

Here some exciting music begins, changing into a poetic Andante and concluding in a majestic motif. (64 bars.)

Change of Scene. The Fir Forest in Winter.

28 Snow begins to fall. Suddenly a snowstorm occurs. Light white snowflakes blow about (60 dancers).

They circle everlastingly to a 3/4 valse.

They form snowballs, a snowdrift, but at a strong gust of wind, the drift breaks up and becomes a circle of dancers.

The End

The snowflakes fall, larger and larger and are lit by electric light.

Tableau

For No. 28 and encircling Valse: during the 3/4 valse a strong gust of wind breaks the dancers into a circle.

Act II

(On a rough copy of the manuscript in the margin, Petipa had written: 'This is what I sent to Monsieur Tchaikovsky in Paris on March 9th, 1891, I have conquered all difficulties.')

(THE PALACE OF THE SUGARPLUM KINGDOM)
Very Fantastic Decor.

1 For the beginning of the Act before the rising of the curtain—

an overture which changes with the rising of the curtain to No. 2 and becomes more grandiose.

The backdrop and wings represent gold

The Nutcracker Prince leads Clara to the land of the Sugarplum Fairy in Act II of Ballet West's production choreographed by Willam Christensen after Petipa-Ivanov.

and silver palms—tinsel or tulle. In the background are fountains of lemonade, orangeade, almond milk and currant syrup.

2   *Andante quasi allegretto of 16 bars, which goes into No. 3.*
In the middle of these fountains, on a river of rose-colored water, is seen a Pavilion of sugar-candy with transparent columns, where the Sugarplum Fairy and her retinue are seen.

At the rising of the curtain, caramels, marzipan, gingerbread, cinnamon, nut cakes, sugarplums, barley sugar, peppermints, lollipops, almonds, raisins, pistachios, almond cakes and little silver-coated soldiers (the Palace sentries), are found on the stage.

3   *The music becomes delicate and harmonious during a further 16 bars.*
In the middle of the stage, stands a little man in a costume of gold brocade.

4   Should I have arpeggios here?
The music broadens and swells, like a gathering storm. A quicker Andante until the end of this part from 24 to 36 bars.
The river of rose-colored water begins to swell visibly and on its stormy surface appear Clara and the handsome Prince on a chariot of shells, studded with stones, glittering in the sun and accompanied by enormous golden dolphins with upraised heads. They ride above the pillars of the flashing rose-colored streams of water, which descend and break into all colors of the rainbow. Six charming Moors, with sunshades hung with bells, in head-dresses made of golden shells and in costumes decorated with humming bird feathers, land and unfold an elegant carpet, which is all studded with peppermints, along which the Prince and his bride make their entrance. The Sugarplum Fairy meets them. The silver-coated soldiers present arms. All the fantastic people make a deep bow. The little man in gold brocade bows low before the Nutcracker crying:—'Oh! dear Prince, at last you are here! Welcome to the Sugarplum Kingdom!'

5   *For this entrance, fairly stormy 3/4, 24 to 32 bars.*
Twelve little pages appear, carrying in their arms lighted aromatic herbs, like torches; their heads are like pearls. The bodies of six of them are made of rubies, the other six are made of emeralds, but in spite of this, they move gracefully on their two little shoes made of fine gold filigree work. Behind them follow four ladies of the height of dolls, but much more splendidly dressed and so richly decorated that Clara recognizes immediately they are the Princesses of the Sugarplum Kingdom. All four of them on seeing the Nutcracker, throw themselves round his neck with genuine sincerity and cry simultaneously, 'Oh! my Prince, Oh! my dear Prince, Oh! my brother, Oh! my dear brother.'

6   *8 bars of a broad and exciting 2/4, then 16 bars of martial music.*
The Nutcracker is deeply moved and taking Clara by the hand, he turns to the

Princesses with emotion and says: 'My dear sisters, this is Mademoiselle Clara Zilberhaus, I wish to present her to you. She saved my life; that is, if she had not thrown her shoe at the Mouse King at the very moment when I was losing the battle, then I should now be lying in my grave or, what is still worse, would have been eaten up by the Mouse King.'

7 *Here the broad 2/4 becomes quick and animated with joy at the freeing of the Nutcracker. 16 bars.*
'Oh! dear Mademoiselle Zilberhaus, Oh! noble savior of our dear beloved Prince and brother.'

8 *Also 2/4. The trumpets of the little silver soldiers are heard. 8 bars and 8 bars in order to allow 'Chocolate' a moment of introduction for the dance.*
The Sugarplum Fairy makes a sign and on the stage, as if by magic, appears a table covered with jellies, etc: The little man commands 'Chocolate' to appear.

Divertissement

9 First Dance.
Chocolate.
Spanish Dance 3/4 from 64 to 80 bars.

10 Second Dance.
Coffee. Arabian, the Kingdom of Yemen.
Coffee Mocha.
Eastern Dance from 24 to 32 bars of cloying and bewitching music.

11 Third Dance.
Tea.
Allegretto of the Chinese type, little bells, etc: 48 bars.

12 Fourth Dance.
Trepak, for the end of the dance, turning on the floor. (Obrouchky)
Quick 2/4—64 bars.

13 Fifth Dance.
Dance of the Flutes.
Tempo Polka, 64 to 90 bars.
They dance, playing on little pipes made of reed, with bobbles on the ends.

14 Sixth Dance.
Dance of 32 Buffoons, with Mère Gigogne and her little children climbing out of her skirts at the head.

64 bars, 2/4 accentuated rhythm, not fast, which combines with 48 bars, 3/4 for the entrance of Mère Gigogne and her children, jumping out of her skirt. Then 2/4 becoming much quicker, from 32 to 48 bars.
At the end a group with Mère Gigogne in the middle of the Buffoons.
A Grand Ballabile!

15 Seventh Dance.
Valse des Fleurs and with large garlands.
8 bars for the start of the waltz, then, the same amount of bars as in the rural waltz in The Sleeping Beauty *(second scene).*
The little man claps his hands and 36 *danseurs* and 36 *danseuses* appear, dressed like flowers who carry a large bouquet and present it to the Prince and his Bride. As soon as this is done, the dancers, as is usual in operas, take their positions and begin to dance.

16 Eighth Dance. *Pas de Deux.*
The Sugarplum Fairy and the handsome Prince.
An Adagio with colossal effects, 48 bars. Variation for the cavalier, 6/8, 48 bars. Variation for the ballerina—plucked strings, 2/4, 32 bars, during which the water can be heard, splashing in the fountain. Then to finish 24 bars very accelerando. Coda another 88 bars— quick 2/4.

17 Ninth Dance.
A Grand General Coda for everyone on the stage including those who have already appeared in their dances.
128 bars 3/4, very brilliant and ardent.

18 Tenth Dance.
Multicolored fountains. Lighted fountains, etc.: etc:
Grandiose Andante from 16 to 24 bars.

THE END

Illustration by Bertall for Dumas' adaptation of Hoffmann's story of the Nutcracker.

*(On the back of the MSS, Petipa wrote in pencil: '29 February, I have written this; it works very well.') (J'ai écrit cela; c'est très bon.)

On 9 March 1891 Tchaikovsky completed the Snowflake Waltz, then set the score aside to travel to America, breaking the journey with a short stay in Paris. The composer had been asked to conduct the opening ceremonies on 5 May 1891 for a new concert auditorium in New York City built by the industrialist and philanthropist, Andrew Carnegie. Then called simply the Music Hall, it has since come to be known as Carnegie Hall. Tchaikovsky prolonged his American visit by agreeing to undertake a short tour as guest conductor, after which he returned to his Russian home at Froklovskoye, where he finished the first draft of *The Nutcracker* on 7 July 1891. He did not begin work on the orchestration until January of 1892, but by March the orchestration was completed and Vsevolojsky received the finished composition on 23 March.

Tchaikovsky's attitudes toward the composition varied wildly, depending upon his mood. If the act of composing had banished his initial lack of interest, the completion of the score left him depressed. 'And now it is finished, *Casse-Noisette* is all ugliness,' he wrote to his brother Modeste, while to his nephew Vladimir Davidov he confided that

Illustration by Bertall. The toys in Fritz's and Mary's cupboard come to life when the army of mice invade at midnight.

he considered it 'infinitely worse' than his other ballets. Yet when faced with the task of completing *Iolanta*, he wrote to his brother that he thought it 'strange that when I was composing the ballet I kept thinking that it wasn't very good but that I would show them [the Imperial Theaters] what I can do when I began the opera. And now it seems that the ballet is good and the opera not so good.'

Tchaikovsky ought to have known that his ballet music was far from the disaster he feared it was. Before the ballet had even been performed in its entirety, he extracted a suite of passages from the score and conducted them on 19 March 1892 at a concert of the Russian Musical Society which also included the premiere of his *Romeo and Juliet*. The ballet excerpts proved so much to the public's liking that five of the numbers had to be encored. This set of pieces is today known as the Nutcracker Suite (Opus 71A) and is very possibly the most familiar ballet music in the world. A best seller in the days of 78 rpm records (the brevity of the numbers making it easy to fit them on record sides without awkward breaks in the middle of the music), it remains a best seller today when the suite can be neatly accommodated on a single side of a long-playing record. The suite is so popular that many newcomers to ballet think that Nutcracker Suite is also the ballet's title and are surprised to find that it is not. They are also usually delighted to discover that the full ballet contains an abundance of unfamiliar melodies as charming as those Tchaikovsky selected for his suite.

Despite the success of this musical preview of the complete ballet, a disastrous situation developed which could have led to the postponement or the outright cancellation of the ballet. In the autumn of 1892 Petipa became ill, so seriously ill that his physician prescribed extended bed rest, thereby making it impossible for him to finish choreographing *The Nutcracker*. Rather than delay the ballet, Petipa entrusted the task of choreographing it to his assistant, Lev Ivanov, provided that Ivanov follow the production scheme which Petipa had conceived and for which Tchaikovsky had composed his music. This delegation of authority has led dance historians ever since to wonder how much of the original production was by Petipa and how much was by Ivanov.

There is no doubt that Ivanov possessed genius. Shortly after Tchaikovsky's death when the Maryinsky Ballet decided to mount an entirely new version of *Swan Lake* in his memory, it was Ivanov who choreographed the ballet's lyrical second and fourth acts—choreography which is still admired today for its tenderness and beauty. Ivanov (1834–1901) choreographed comparatively little during his long theatrical career, and remains one of the enigmas of nineteenth-century Russian ballet. He was a product of the St Petersburg Imperial Ballet School (whose ledger bluntly lists him as an 'illegitimate son': such children were often sent as boarding students to the State theatrical or dance schools where they could receive a good education and train for a rewarding career, while at the same time remain away from any home environment where their presence might prove an embarrassment). Admitted into the Maryinsky Ballet in 1850, Ivanov revealed himself to be an unusually musical dancer, excelling in both noble classical and character roles. It was also discovered that he had a pedagogical flair, and he started teaching classes in 1858. As Petipa's assistant, he worked with the choreographer on several productions, occasionally creating dances for which Petipa himself later took the credit.

Some partisans of Russian ballet accuse the foreign-born Petipa of deliberately trying to minimize the abilities of the Russian-born Ivanov. It also seems true that Ivanov made no unusual, concerted efforts to assert himself. If he were forever in Petipa's shadow, he did not attempt to escape into his own sunlight. People remember Ivanov as a fine teacher and a genial, slightly lackadaisical man fond of good music and perhaps a bit too fond of good wine. He loved the Maryinsky and its traditions and often expressed the wish that he could die 'in harness' rather than waste away in unproductive old age. The wish was granted. One day,

after rehearsing Delibes' *Sylvia*, he was stricken with a seizure and died soon afterwards.

What is probably most fair to say of *The Nutcracker* is that it is Ivanov's choreography based upon Petipa's concepts. Tchaikovsky attended rehearsals of the ballet, sometimes serving as rehearsal pianist. Some historians believe that Ivanov was inspired by Tchaikovsky's music but thwarted by the necessity of having to tailor his own creative ideas to fit Petipa's plans. Trying to choreograph a Jester's dance (to the piece of music familiarly known as the Trepak), Ivanov became stuck and ran out of ideas. Alexander Shiryaev who portrayed the Jester therefore had to invent his own steps for the dance.

Nevertheless rehearsals proceeded, and *The Nutcracker* and *Iolanta* eventually shared a bill together as planned. The opera concerns the blind daughter of a king. Out of kindness to her, no one has ever told her that she is blind or has let her feel that she is in any way different from other people. A doctor informs her father that her blindness is curable: the conditions for her cure, however, are, first, she must realize that she is blind and, secondly, she must desire to see. But the king prefers to let Iolanta live in blissful ignorance. A young man inadvertently tells her that she is blind, that she is not the same as everyone else. The king, enraged, seeks to have the youth executed, but Iolanta begs that he be spared, saying that she would do anything to help this young man whose voice so entranced her. The preconditions for her cure have now been met. After wishing to see the young man she desires to aid, she gains her sight and the opera ends happily with their marriage.

The first performance of *The Nutcracker* and *Iolanta* at the Maryinsky was the *répétition générale* of 17 December 1892. Literally translated *répétition générale* means 'general rehearsal' (and, by implication, 'dress rehearsal'). In the theaters of France and Russia at the end of the nineteenth century the term meant more than that and the event was far more than a rehearsal. The *répétition générale* was a gala preview performance to which

Right
Tchaikovsky's study at Klin.
Inset
Portrait of P I Tchaikovsky by the artist Kuznetsov.

Above
The Sugarplum Fairy
rewards Clara and the
Nutcracker Prince with
sweets and entertain-
ment including the
Waltz of the Flowers in
a Cincinnati Ballet
production.
Left
Terry Hayworth as
Drosselmeyer and
Manelle Jaye as Clara
watch the three
Mirlitons (Cheryl Liss,
Carole Hill, Vivien
Loeber) during the
divertissements in Act II
of the London Festival
Ballet production.

Above
Drosselmeyer presents
his special gifts for the
children, which include
two dancing German
dolls and two life-size
performing poodle dogs
(Cincinnati Ballet).
Far right
On their way to the
Kingdom of Sweets
Clara and the Nutcracker
Prince journey through
the Land of Snow and
the Snowflakes dance
for them (Cincinnati
Ballet).
Right
In the Ballet West
production Mother
Buffoon appears in
Act II along with her
many children.

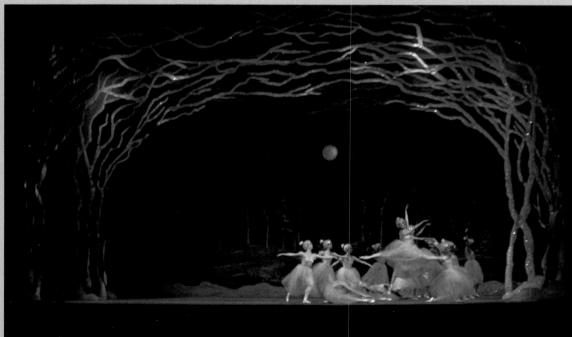

Left and right
Members of the Cincinnati Ballet Company in the Waltz of the Flowers, Act II.
Below
In the Cincinnati Ballet production Mère Gigogne is called Mother Ginger. Clara watches as her children appear from under her skirts.

the theater director would invite critics, public figures, and members of high society, not only to ascertain their reactions to a new production, but in the hopes that they would also talk about it afterward and stir up such interest in it that audiences would flock to the regular public performances.

The *répétition générale* was conducted by the Maryinsky's chief conductor, Riccardo Drigo, himself a successful composer of ballet music. Designed by M I Botcharov and K M Ivanov, with costumes by Vsevolojsky, *The Nutcracker* starred Antoniette dell'Era, a guest ballerina from Italy, as the Sugarplum Fairy. Throughout the nineteenth century, while France and Russia produced great choreographers, Italian ballet schools turned out dazzling technicians. Italian guest stars were especially popular in Russia, where they amazed audiences with their prodigies of virtuosity and encouraged Russian ballerinas to increase their own technical proficiency in order to be able to hold their own with them. Dell'Era's cavalier was Pavel Gerdt, for years the most distinguished male dancer in Russian ballet. In

1892 he was 48 and past his prime as a technician, but he remained a noble presence and a superb partner. The Drosselmeyer was veteran character dancer Timofei Stukolkin and the cast of 200 (augmented for the occasion by boys from the military school attached to the Finnish Guard Regiment, in the roles of mice) contained many notable dancers. Gustav and Nicholas Legat (father and son and members of a famous Russian family of dancers) appeared in the Grandfather Dance. Nicholas Legat, who later became a distinguished teacher, was also cast in the Chinese Dance with Mathilde Kschessinska, who was shortly to reveal herself to be the most spectacular technician Russian ballet had thus far produced. Kschessinska is also important to political as well as ballet history, for she was the mistress of Tsar Nicholas II before his accession to the throne and after the Revolution she married his cousin, the Grand Duke André. When the Bolsheviks gained power, it was from the balcony of Kschessinska's house that Lenin made his first public speech. After her retirement as a dancer Kschessinska

Left
The Sugarplum Fairy and her cavalier dance for Clara during her visit to the Kingdom of Sweets (Cincinnati Ballet Company).
Below
Mademoiselle Mathilde Kschessinska, the great Russian dancer, made her debut at Covent Garden in London in the week of 18 November 1911.

became a well-regarded teacher in Paris. So did another Russian ballerina, Olga Preobrajenska, who played a clockwork doll in the original *Nutcracker*.

Like most productions today, Ivanov's production told the story of Clara's Christmas Eve adventures in the first act, the act ending with her journey through the Land of Snow. The second act consisted of the festivities in her honor in the Kingdom of Sweets. Near the beginning of the second act occurred an incident still retained in some stagings. This is a mime scene in which the Nutcracker Prince tells the Sugarplum Fairy all that happened to him and to Clara. Not simply a form of realistic dramatic gesture, mime in the old Imperial Russian ballet was a formalized sign language almost as complex as the sign language of the deaf, in which each gesture was assigned a special meaning. The mime scene in *The Nutcracker* became one of the most famous of all such scenes. The New York City Ballet production includes it, and critic Edwin Denby summarizes it in this fashion: when the Fairy asks the Prince where they are from, the little Prince gestures, 'We come from way over there. This is what happened. I was sleeping. The mice attacked. I fought them. I fought the Mouse King. And Clara threw her shoe and saved me. I killed the Mouse King. This is what happened.' And the Fairy gestures, 'You have a brave heart.'

The remainder of the second act was devoted to the *divertissement*. A popular feature of most Russian ballets of the time, the *divertissement* was a suite of dances bearing no direct connection with the development of the dramatic action, inserted into a ballet simply to show off the company's dancers. The *divertissement* usually came near the end of a ballet, frequently during the last act, where it brought the production to a festive conclusion after all the threads of the story had been tied together. Ivanov's *divertissement* included dances which suggested foreign countries and things to eat and drink. Dancers represented hot chocolate from Spain, coffee from Arabia, and tea from China. There was also a Trepak, a lusty Russian folk dance. George Balanchine's pro-

duction for the New York City Ballet makes this a dance for some spirited candy canes, and Balanchine says that the choreography is as he remembers it from his own youthful days at the Maryinsky. In other productions, which also claim Russian sources, this is a dance for Russian clowns. Further *divertissement* numbers include the perennially popular Waltz of the Flowers, a dance for reed flutes (the *mirlitons*), and the entry of a comic figure of a woman in an enormous skirt from under which hordes of tiny children emerge.

The climax of the *divertissement* is the *grand pas de deux*, a duet for the ballerina and the *premier danseur*. In Russian ballet the sections which comprised the *pas de deux* followed a prescribed order. The adagio featured slow sustained movements for both dancers. Then came solos, termed variations, for each dancer, the male variation preceding that of the ballerina. Finally in the coda the two stars danced together again, their movements this time being quick and bright. The *Nutcracker pas de deux* was for the Sugarplum Fairy and her Prince, and one of the peculiarities of the way that ballet is constructed is that this is virtually all the dancing these characters do in the entire ballet. Ivanov was to be seriously criticized for this, and later choreographers have often tried hard to devise ways to expand the ballerina's role.

The Russian name of the Fairy's prince has puzzled many Western ballet students. The prince is called Prince Koklush, and everyone who knows a little Russian soon discovers, with bewilderment, that Koklush means 'whooping cough.' Why should a prince in a children's fairy tale be called Whooping Cough—especially since, a century ago, whooping cough was not a malady to be taken lightly? Scholars familiar with the intricacies of foreign slang, however, know that at one time Koklush meant something other than whooping cough. The Russian word derives from the French *coqueluche*, which in addition to its medical meaning can refer to a hooded bonnet of the Middle Ages worn by fashionable gentle-

men. So used, the term gave rise to such phrases as *coqueluche de la ville* (town dandy) and *coqueluche des dames* (ladies' man)—and this is surely the sort of *coqueluche* Prince Koklush is meant to be, although no one is sure why this term has such totally disparate meanings.

After the *pas de deux* Ivanov brought *The Nutcracker* to an end with a dance in which all the *divertissement* soloists returned to dance together with the ensemble. This in turn was followed by an allegorical apotheosis in which a beehive guarded by flying bees symbolized civilization with its productive work and commerce.

Present at the *répétition générale* was Tsar Alexander III himself, who seemed visibly pleased and called Tchaikovsky into his box to congratulate him. Tchaikovsky, after his months of self-doubt, also seemed pleased. If anything, he thought the production 'too magnificent—the eye gets tired of so much gorgeousness.' Other observers, however, including the critics, were less elated. *Iolanta* enjoyed a *succès d'estime*, but was considered unnecessarily long. *The Nutcracker* prompted considerable sniping. Although, as excerpted for a suite, Tchaikovsky's music had met with approval, the complete score may have been too subtle to reveal all its charm in a single hearing (a fate which also befell the score of *The Sleeping Beauty* at its premiere two years earlier). In any case the music disappointed some balletgoers, as did the ballerina, dell'Era. Though technically able, she was apparently devoid of charm, Modeste Tchaikovsky pronouncing her 'too heavy and unattractive' as the Sugarplum Fairy.

The scenario and choreography were also found wanting. Modeste attributed some of the production's weaknesses to Ivanov's limitations as a choreographer, saying, 'When it was only a matter of dancing, he [Ivanov] fulfilled his task magnificently, but the action scenes were a total flop, especially the war between the mice and the toys. . . .' Some years after the premiere the respected critic Konstantin Skalkovsky expressed in his book, *The Theatre World*, the views of many balletgoers at the time: 'Generally speaking, *The Nutcracker* was staged mainly for children; for the dancers it contains very little; for art—exactly nothing.'

One of the unhappy balletgoers present at the Maryinsky was the twenty-two-year-old artist Alexandre Benois. Benois (1870–1960) was an ardent lover of ballet; more than that, believing ballet could be a great art as well as an entertaining diversion, he championed attempts at truly serious ballet. Early in our own century, he became one of the progressive young artists and composers who collaborated on the innovative productions of the Diaghilev Ballet. In 1890 Benois had praised *The Sleeping Beauty* and he had hoped that *The Nutcracker* would be as fine. But *The Nutcracker* was a cruel disappointment for him. Dismayed by its décor and music, the young painter wrote in his diary: '*Casse-Noisette* has not turned out a success! And

it was just in this ballet that I had placed all my hopes, knowing Tchaikovsky's talent for creating a fairy-tale atmosphere . . . . The décor of Scene I is both disgusting and profoundly shocking . . . stupid, coarse, heavy and dark. . . . The second act is still worse . . . while at times the music reminds one of an open-air military band. Tchaikovsky has never written anything more banal than these numbers!'

Over the years, Benois modified these opinions, growing increasingly fond of *The Nutcracker*, and later in his life he even designed several productions of the ballet. In 1892, however, the only portions of the work in which he detected merit were the Trepak, the Tea and Coffee dances and the *pas de deux*. Most of the critics agreed with him about the *pas de deux*, with its stately,

The grandmother joins the dancing at the Christmas party in the production by the Boston Ballet Company.

smoothly flowing adagio and its delicate variation for the Sugarplum Fairy. A version of it still exists and is employed in some productions, generations of dancers having taught it to each other. Since no universally accepted system of dance notation exists, this is how almost all choreography is preserved. While dancers' memories are often astonishingly good, they are also, like all memories, fallible, and one can only speculate about how accurate those *Nutcracker pas de deux* are which claim to be 'after Ivanov.' Still the *pas de deux* remains one of the few bits of Ivanov choreography for *The Nutcracker* which have survived.

One other scene from the ballet, as choreographed by Ivanov, also received lavish praise at the premiere. This was the dance for the Snowflakes at the end of the first act.

An ensemble dance of symphonic proportions, it required a *corps de ballet* of 60 women, plus eight female soloists. In this choreographic impression of a snowstorm, the masses of dancers formed intricate patterns suggesting falling and drifting snow; at one moment, the dancers assembled in the form of a star; at another, they bunched together as though rolled up in a gigantic snowball, and at the end they came to a sudden halt, as though driven by the wind into a snowdrift. To increase the wintry illusion, the dancers carried wands with flakes attached to them on wires which quivered as they moved, while tiny snowballs were attached to their headpieces, also on vibrating wires. The Snowflakes' dance became a great favorite of the entrenched balletomanes who always tried to view it from one of the upper balconies, where the choreographic patterns stood out with unusual clarity.

Some historians and critics believe that Ivanov was able to create so distinctively in this scene because he was not hampered by the demands of a plot which he had not helped to devise. Their view supports the theory that Ivanov suffered by having to force his own choreography into a framework established by someone else. Almost from the day after the premiere, people started tinkering with *The Nutcracker*, hoping to make it better. It is hard to imagine that some of the changes were improvements: for instance, in an effort to expand the ballerina role at later performances of the ballet, dell'Era interpolated a gavotte composed by Alphonse Czibulka, a Hungarian pianist and composer of sentimental salon music. Czibulka's tunes are sweet enough, and one of them, 'Love's Dream After the Ball,' is sometimes learned by piano students, even today. Surely Czibulka's gavotte did not harmonize with Tchaikovsky, however effective it may have been as a showpiece for dell'Era.

As a result of constant changes, most of Ivanov's choreography has been lost over the years. What has remained is Tchaikovsky's music which, though it may have made little impression upon its first-night audience, has continued to gain in popularity.

Tchaikovsky's Music

Even his detractors concede that Peter Ilyitch Tchaikovsky could write music which sounds effective in the theater. Tchaikovsky's sure sense of climax and his mastery of orchestral color help make his music inherently dramatic. Moreover the special requirements of opera and ballet help conceal one of his principal weaknesses as a composer. Tchaikovsky could not always develop thematic materials at great length or sustain them in large-scale forms. For this reason a body of critical opinion holds that his symphonies and concertos are structurally flawed. However, since operas and ballets, at least the typical operas and ballets of Tchaikovsky's day, consist of a series of individual arias or dances, Tchaikovsky was able to write one fine melody after another without having to worry constantly about developing these melodies symphonically.

To some degree Tchaikovsky's melodies reflect his cosmopolitan leanings. Unlike other nineteenth-century Russian composers such as Mussorgsky, Borodin, Rimsky-Korsakov, and Balakirev, who made a point of their nationalism, Tchaikovsky, though very much a Russian, was also an internationalist in his musical taste. His style derives from French sources in particular. He was so fond of French music that he

Drosselmeyer's mechanical dolls perform for the guests (American Ballet Theater).

even professed to rate French composers some critics would term minor figures above the lofty German symphonists of his time, professing a special love for Bizet, Massenet, Delibes, Guiraud, Lalo, Godard, and Saint-Saëns. He admired these composers for their melodic sense and craftsmanship, and also, perhaps, for their modesty and sense of propriety, for their refusal to be pompous or bombastic. The composer he loved most, however, was not French. Tchaikovsky adored Mozart. Again what he responded to in Mozart was his melodic power and his ability to hold all elements of a musical composition in perfect balance and proportion. As music critic Edward Lockspeiser remarked, 'It must surely have been a Mozart of Dresden china that he worshipped.'

These tastes help account for the fastidiousness of many of Tchaikovsky's compositions, but, as Lockspeiser has also observed, there can be 'an almost hysterical emotionalism' to his music. On more than one occasion, Tchaikovsky's musical Dresden china is shattered by the force of passion. He even subtitled his sixth symphony the *Pathétique*. Biographers fond of psychological theories speculate that such juxtapositions of delicate restraint and emotional outpouring may have their origins in Tchaikovsky's unhappy life. Regarded in purely musical terms, these juxtapositions help explain why his scores sound so dramatic.

Tchaikovsky wrote only three ballets: *Swan Lake*, *The Sleeping Beauty*, and *The Nutcracker*. Yet those three rank among the greatest ballet scores of all time, and many balletgoers believe that they are equalled only by the ballet scores which Igor Stravinsky (himself an admirer of Tchaikovsky) wrote in our own century. What is even more remarkable is that dozens of choreographers have set ballets to music by Tchaikovsky which was not originally written to be danced. Tchaikovsky may well be the world's most often danced to composer. The works which choreographers have chosen are remarkable for their sheer variety. One

Left
The Harlequin and Columbine in Act I of the London Festival Ballet production.
Below
In the Ballet West production choreographed by Willam Christensen, the dancing dolls which Drosselmeyer brings to the Stahlbaum's party include a ballerina doll and a furry brown bear.

might expect that Tchaikovsky's vivid tone poems would inspire David Lichine, Robert Helpmann and Serge Lifar to choreograph dramatic ballets to *Francesca da Rimini*, *Hamlet*, and *Romeo and Juliet* respectively. *Romeo and Juliet* in particular has attracted choreographers. Among those choreographers other than Lifar who have tried to tell Shakespeare's story to Tchaikovsky's music are Alberto Alonso, Willam Christensen, and George Skibine. One might also expect that Isadora Duncan, always the champion of political and artistic freedom, might find the Marche Slave suitable accompaniment for a dance about a chained slave struggling to break her fetters. In addition to using scores with programmatic content or implications, choreographers have employed Tchaikovsky's concertos, chamber music, and symphonies for their ballets. Herbert Ross has choreographed the violin concerto, Dennis Nahat has choreographed the sextet, Gerald Arpino set his *Reflections* to the Variations on a Rococo Theme for Violincello and Orchestra, and John Clifford and Jacques d'Amboise choreographed the first and second orchestral suites. The A-minor trio inspired two radically different ballets. To the theme and variations movement alone, in its original scoring, John Taras choreographed the lyrical and plotless *Designs With Strings*, while to an orchestration of the complete work Léonide Massine choreographed *Aleko*, a tempestuous dance-drama inspired by Pushkin's *The Gypsies*. Kenneth Mac-Millan used the first and third symphonies for his ballet about the Russian Revolution, *Anastasia*; Isadora Duncan danced to the sixth symphony; and Massine's *Les Présages* (to the fifth symphony), a vast allegory about man and his destiny, was one of the most controversial ballets of the 1930s. Other ballets employ assorted compositions by Tchaikovsky. Lew Christensen's *Beauty and the Beast* is set to a potpourri of orchestral selections. Benjamin Harkarvy's *Time Passed Summer* mixes Tchaikovsky songs with electronic sounds devised by Charles Cohen. John Cranko's *Eugene Onegin*, telling the same Pushkin-derived story as one of Tchaikovsky's operas, utilizes various short pieces, but not a note of any of the opera music.

Of all twentieth-century choreographers, it is George Balanchine, creator of an influential *Nutcracker* production, who has probably turned most often to Tchaikovsky's concert music. In 1934 his danced version of the *Serenade* for string orchestra made history as his first ballet choreographed in America. Over the years he has set the second and third

piano concertos (under the titles of *Ballet Imperial* and *Allegro Brillante*), the *Meditation* for violin and piano, and third and the fourth orchestral suites—the latter under the title of *Mozartiana*, which was Tchaikovsky's own subtitle for this tribute to his favorite composer—as well as the third symphony, which has become the Diamonds sequence of the three-part *Jewels*.

Tchaikovsky's music—including the music not originally written for dancing—has attracted many choreographers because it fulfills two important requirements of ballet music. First of all, even in the most solemn of the symphonies, there is always a strongly perceptible pulse, a pulse which varies from section to section within a composition, thereby providing rhythmic life and avoiding monotony. Secondly Tchaikovsky's music is vivid music. It makes a strong impression in the theater, and dancers find it easy to retain in their memories.

In his own lifetime Tchaikovsky was accused of having a predilection for ballet music. Since ballet music in those days was not held in high esteem by many composers, this was considered a serious failing. Thus in a letter Tchaikovsky's friend and fellow composer Sergei Taneyev chided him about the fourth symphony, saying that 'in every movement there are phrases which sound like ballet music—the middle section of the andante, the trio of the scherzo and a kind of marche in the finale. Hearing the symphony, my inner eye sees involuntarily our prima ballerina which puts me out of humor and spoils my pleasure in the many beauties of the work.'

Tchaikovsky readily admitted the balletic qualities of his symphonic compositions but, fortunately for generations of balletgoers to come, he refused to mend his musical ways, remarking that he could 'never understand why "ballet-music" should be used as a con-

temptuous epithet. The music of a ballet is not invariably bad, there are good works of this class—Delibes' *Sylvia*, for instance.' Believing that ballet music could be a distinguished genre, Tchaikovsky took his own ballet projects seriously, composing works which are not only eminently danceable but also agreeable to listen to independent of dancing.

The Nutcracker Suite, for instance, is as popular on records or in the concert hall as the complete *Nutcracker* ballet is on stage. Curiously Tchaikovsky was not the only composer who set Hoffmann's story to music. That story became the basis for a suite of piano pieces, Nussknacker und Mausekönig (Opus 46) by Karl Reinecke (1824-1910), a German composer largely unknown today but respected in his lifetime for his symphonic and children's music and also for the editions which he prepared of Beethoven's piano sonatas. More curiously still Reinecke also wrote music inspired by the tale of *The Sleeping Beauty*.

Tchaikovsky's *The Nutcracker* is divided into an overture and 15 sections (several of which are subdivided still further). In this account those numbers which were included in the Nutcracker Suite are marked with an asterisk. The rustling *overture, which begins pianissimo, is the first of the score's marvels. Its unusual delicacy derives from the absence of cellos and double basses; therefore no dark string tones can spoil the exquisite shimmer of the music. Exemplary in purely musical terms, the overture is also admirably conceived theatrically. It surrounds a production from the very start with an aura of magic. Music critic Robert Lawrence quite rightly says, 'Those who have heard the prelude in the concert suite alone can have little idea of the heightened effect induced by the glow of the footlights, the darkened theater. This is music written in terms of the stage.' Borrowing his imagery from the eatables which figure so prominently in the ballet, Lincoln Kirstein, Director of the New York City Ballet, once described the overture as 'a delicate miniature, an apéritif . . . to the banquet which is to come.'

The unhappy Clara is comforted while Anton Dolin as Drosselmeyer examines her broken nutcracker.

After the overture the curtain rises upon

Act I

1 *Scène (allegro non troppo—poco più sostenuto —più moderato—allegro vivace—meno)*

This scene concerns the decoration and lighting of the Christmas tree, the arrival of the party guests, and the showing of the illuminated tree to the children. Tchaikovsky has filled the episode with several pictorial effects. A repeated rhythmic figure heard at the very outset suggests the happy anticipation of the children. Once they see the tree, their awe is expressed by an oboe phrase supported by string tremolandi and harp.

*2 *Marche (tempo di marcia viva)*

The children assemble for a little march. Since these marchers are only children, the march is unusually light in texture, disdaining brass band effects.

3 *Petit Galop des Enfants et Entrée des Parents (presto-andante—allegro)*

The children dance and their parents join in. One of the tunes Tchaikovsky uses here is that of an old French song, which wishes a certain Mr. Dumollet a safe voyage without shipwreck: '*Bon voyage, cher Dumollet, à Saint Malo débarquez sans naufrage!*' This is the first of several old popular songs or folk tunes which appear in *The Nutcracker*. The dance comes to an abrupt halt. Why? The answer is given in

4 *Scène Dansante (andantino—allegro vivo— andante sostenuto—più andante—allegro molto vivace—molto più presto—tempo di valse— presto)*

The entrance of Drosselmeyer, simultaneously comic and faintly ominous, is indicated by the violas and tenor trombone. The score almost persuades one to picture Drosselmeyer stepping forward while the children

Right
Leslie Brown as Clara in the American Ballet Theater production choreographed by Mikhail Baryshnikov. In his version the children's roles are filled by adult dancers.
Below
The adults join the dancing at the Stahlbaum's Christmas party (American Ballet Theater).

shrink back, just a little bit scared. Drosselmeyer brings presents with him, among them two dancing clockwork dolls. Productions differ as to what these dolls represent, yet they are always dolls of contrasting sorts, for Tchaikovsky assigns them contrasting music. The first doll dances to a gentle waltz, while the second is given a ferocious *presto*.

5 *Scène et Danse du Grossvater (andante—poco animando—andantino—più mosso—moderato assai—andante—lo stesso tempo—più mosso—tempo I—lo stesso tempo—tempo di grossvater)*

The music follows the narrative of Petipa's scenario. Drosselmeyer gives Clara the nutcracker, her brother wants the toy for himself, runs off with it, and breaks it by trying to stuff too large a nut into the nutcracker's jaws. The music which has grown increasingly rapid and feverish breaks off here, then turns slow and tender as Clara weeps over her toy and Drosselmeyer tries to repair it.

Tchaikovsky's next tune sounds like a lullaby, and that is just exactly what it is. The little girls at the party are playing with their

Above
Nathalia Makarova dancing in the role of Clara for the American Ballet Theater.
Right
Leslie Brown as Clara and Gayle Young as Drosselmeyer in the American Ballet Theater production.

dolls, getting ready to put them to bed. Trumpet tootles and drum clatters interrupt them as little boys stomp about, making a nuisance of themselves. Again the little girls cradle their dolls to the lullaby, and once more the quiet is shattered by the mischievous boys. Their elders restrain the miscreants and the stage is cleared for the *Danse du Grossvater*. The Grandfather (Grossvater) Dance traditionally brought parties to an end, just as in America earlier in our century playing 'Good Night, Ladies' indicated that this was the last dance, after which the musicians would pack up their instruments and depart. Young and old alike join in the Grossvater, which is danced to a traditional melody in two parts, each of which can be repeated indefinitely according to the pleasure of the musicians and party guests; it has a rather stately opening theme, followed by a brisker, skipping figure. Tchaikovsky was not the first composer to have incorporated the Grossvater theme into a piece of music, Robert Schumann having made use of it in Papillons and Carnaval, and both compositions evoke parties of one sort or another.

6 *Scène (allegro semplice—moderato con moto—allegro giusto—più allegro—moderato assai)*

The guests leave to a calm melody. The first half—the realistic half—of the first act has ended. What follows is a transition to the world of fantasy. Clara creeps downstairs to be back with her nutcracker. Tremulous sounds in the strings indicate her fear at being alone in the darkened room. The clock strikes midnight. Scurrying sounds signal the arrival of the mice. There begins a spacious melody on violins and harp, and with it the Christmas tree magically begins to grow of its own accord until the melody attains a tremendous climax.

7 *Scène (pochissimo più mosso)*

A master of theatrical contrast and surprise, Tchaikovsky, after breaking off the rich melody symbolizing the magical Christmas tree grown to immense proportions, now returns the listener to the diminutive world of toys with a grotesque figure on the oboes: one of the dolls has perceived the mice and like a sentry is calling out, 'Halt! Who goes there?' When no answer follows, a shot is fired and drums roll. The agitated music for this scene abounds in illustrative touches depicting the battle between the toys and the mice. Calm returns when Clara throws her slipper and the nutcracker turns into a prince.

8 *Scène (andante)*

To a rich flowing melody Clara and her Nutcracker Prince begin their journey into the Land of the Snow. Productions which include a Snow Queen and a Snow King in their cast use this music for their *pas de deux*. In productions in which these characters are omitted, the music often accompanies spectacular scenic effects. For example, in the New York City Ballet's version, Clara's bed begins to move of its own accord here, taking her away into an enchanted dream world.

Clara, unable to sleep
thinking about her nutcracker,
returns to the parlor.
She is frightened by
the dark shadows and
the unexplained noises
(Ballet West).

9 *Valse des Flocons de Neige (tempo di valse—presto—poco meno)*

Now begins the Snowflake Waltz which so delighted audiences at the first performance. The middle section of the composition contains a wordless melody to be sung by a children's chorus. Elaborate stagings sometimes use the chorus as specified, but more modest productions often rescore the vocal parts for instruments. Some productions, able to afford the services of a chorus but unable to have the chorus present at every performance, tape the vocal portions and play the tape when the proper moment occurs in the score. If conductor and tape are perfectly together in tempo, one usually cannot tell whether the singing is live or recorded. Stories are also told of horrendous occasions when the orchestra and the tape have not been properly synchronized—and of the decidedly odd sounds which occur at such times.

Right
In the Royal Winnipeg Ballet Company production of *The Nutcracker* Salvatore Aeillo as Drosselmeyer is a ballet master who gives Maria (Marina Eglevsky) point shoes for her birthday. Maria's brother and fellow cadets give Maria the military doll.
Below
Clara with her nutcracker in a Royal Ballet production.

Act II

Tchaikovsky found this act especially difficult to compose, confessing to his brother, 'I am groping in the dark, finding it impossible to express musically the Sugarplum Kingdom.' Nevertheless the second act contains what is now the most familiar music in the entire ballet.

10 *Scène (andante)*
To a singing melody for harp, violins, and cello, the curtain rises upon the Land of Sweets. Clara and the little Prince arrive, and the Sugarplum Fairy greets them to a passage for trombones and tuba.

11 *Scène (andante con moto—poco animando—allegro agitato—poco più allegro—tempo precedente)*
Little pages help prepare a feast for Clara and the Prince. The Prince then recounts in mime the adventures of Christmas Eve. Tchaikovsky helps make his account easy to follow by

Left
Clara is told that she must share the nutcracker with her brother. In this Vic-Wells Ballet production of 1934 Nicholas Sergueeff adapted the choreography from the early Russian productions which he knew.

Right
In the London Festival Ballet production Clara plays with her new nutcracker while the other little girls play with their Christmas toys.

glockenspiel. The China evoked by this piece is the quaint land of silk and porcelain that existed only in the imaginations of nineteenth-century Europeans.

   *(d) *Trepak (tempo di trepak, molto vivace —prestissimo)*

The Trepak is a vigorous Russian folk dance which gathers momentum as it proceeds.

   *(e) *Les Mirlitons (moderato assai)*

A *mirliton* is a home-made children's musi-

bringing back some of the mouse and battle themes from the first act at appropriate moments in the Prince's story. The story ended, several sets of fanfares announce the beginning of the grand celebration that the Sugarplum Fairy has prepared for the children.

12 *Divertissement*

The suite of dances begins with

   (a) *Le Chocolat (allegro brillante—più mosso)*

Hot chocolate is represented by a Spanish dance with a jaunty melody for the trumpets.

   *(b) *Le Café (commodo)*

Coffee has an Arabian dance, hushed and slightly mysterious. The melody is a folk tune from the region of the Caucasus known as Georgia.

   *(c) *Le Thé (allegro moderato)*

Tea dances to a chuckling staccato rhythm, and the scoring includes a part for the cal instrument consisting of a piece of reed covered at each end with a paper. It produces a piping sound, and the flutes pipe daintily away through Tchaikovsky's composition.

(f) *La Mère Gigogne et les Polichinelles (allegro giocoso—allegro vivo—poco più)*

In French a *gigogne* is a woman with too many children, and Mother Gigogne, surely a relative of the Old Woman Who Lived in a Shoe, arrives with a flock of tiny children concealed beneath the folds of her enormous skirts. Sometimes in American productions, the character is renamed—Mother Ginger and Mother Marshmallow being some of the new names she has been assigned. Mother Gigogne's entrance music is a French folk tune. Later Tchaikovsky incorporates another old French melody into his score, a song which begins, '*Cadet Roussel a trois maisons,*' concerning a little boy with three birdhouses for swallows.

Valse des Fleurs

The Waltz of the Flowers is perhaps the best-known and best-loved piece in all of *The Nutcracker*. Tchaikovsky was a master of the waltz form, and this waltz is regarded by many listeners as one of his very finest. However there have been dissenting opinions about the Waltz of the Flowers. One of them was that of music critic Eric Blom, who pronounced it an example of Tchaikovsky's ballet music 'at its tawdriest . . . ballroom music, not without liveliness, but quite devoid of elegance. It is a dance not of flowers, but of very matter of fact youths and maidens watched over by voluminous duennas and experienced matrons with dishonorable matrimonial intentions.' Hundreds—perhaps thousands—of music lovers and dance-goers will not agree in the least.

14 *Pas de deux*

Following the standard form of the *grand pas de deux*, there are four sections:

(a) *Andante maestoso—poco più mosso—incalzando—animando—tempo I*

The adagio section of the *grand pas de deux* is very grand indeed, with an unusually beautiful melody based upon nothing more complex than a descending scale. A child could easily play this melodic pattern on the piano, yet Tchaikovsky works wonders with it.

(b) *Tempo di Tarantella*

The Prince is given a variation in the form of the Italian folk dance known as the tarantella, although choreography for this piece never deliberately evokes Italy in the same way that the choreography for Hot Chocolate or Tea evokes Spain or China.

*(c) *Andante non troppo—presto*

The Sugarplum Fairy dances to the celesta, a keyboard instrument consisting of steel plates struck by hammers which produce an ethereal tinkling sound. The celesta was one

Right
Marianna Tcherkassky and Mikhail Baryshnikov were featured in the roles of Clara and the Nutcracker Prince in the American Ballet Theater production premiered in 1976.

of Tchaikovsky's discoveries. En route to New York City to conduct the opening concert at Carnegie Hall, Tchaikovsky stopped off in Paris where he visited with Auguste Mustel, a member of a family of inventors of musical instruments. Mustel demonstrated his new pride and joy, the celesta, which Tchaikovsky called 'divinely beautiful.' Although it had been introduced at a public concert in 1886 and the typophone, a similar instrument invented by Auguste Mustel's father, Victor Mustel (founder of the firm of Mustel et ses Fils), had been employed by Charles Widor in the score of the ballet *La Korrigane* presented at the Paris Opéra in 1880, the celesta was still unknown in Russia. Vowing to become the first Russian composer to make use of it, Tchaikovsky purchased one for the equivalent of $240 and ordered it to be shipped back to Russia under conditions of the utmost secrecy, for he feared that Rimsky-Korsakoff or Glazunov might get hold of one before him.

(d) *Vivace assai*

A sparkling coda concludes the *pas de deux*.

15 *Valse Finale et Apothéose (tempo di valse— maesto meno)*

After a waltz the music which accompanies Clara's arrival into the Land of Sweets returns, this time building to a spacious conclusion.

Once one knows the music for *The Nutcracker* one cannot put it out of one's mind. It lodges in the memory and then, as British dance critic Mary Clarke has remarked, it 'seems always to have been part of our consciousness . . . we do not remember it ever being quite new. It tinkles, sparkles and enchants and takes us nearer to the world of the fairy tale than any other music by Tchaikovsky.'

Nutcrackers Around the World

Russia

One of the paradoxes of *The Nutcracker* is that, although it was less than a success at its premiere, it continued to be performed and it continues to be performed today. Some of the more analytically minded among those members of the audience who were dis-gruntled at the first performance raised serious objections to the way Petipa and Ivanov had structured *The Nutcracker*—objections which continue to be raised against the ballet.

The Nutcracker, they complained, is dramaturgically unsatisfactory. The first act is all

Clara and the Nutcracker Prince in the Land of Ice and Snow (London Festival Ballet).

narrative, while the second is all *divertissement*. Balletomanes fond of watching their favorite stars tackle lengthy roles have their own special complaints. *The Nutcracker*, they sigh, just does not give a ballerina enough to do. What appears to be the ballet's leading role—the part of Clara—is merely a child's role, while the ballerina role—that of the Sugarplum Fairy—is disappointingly small, since the Sugarplum Fairy, outside of dancing one *pas de deux* (although admittedly a glorious one) has little to do except be Clara's gracious hostess in the Land of Sweets. Literary minded balletgoers sometimes object that the ballet turns Hoffmann's quirky story into an innocuous entertainment. For them *The Nutcracker* is much too saccharine. British critic A H Franks finds the children in the ballet objectionably sentimentalized. 'All the Claras I can remember,' he says, 'have spent a great deal of their time hunching their shoulders and clasping their hands just under their chin in simulation of childish transportation and delight. In fact excited and transported children spend only a fleeting fraction of their time in such an attitude.'

Producers of *The Nutcracker* have responded in two ways to these arguments. Some, defending Petipa's production scheme, offer versions that attempt to justify the peculiarities of the original scenario. These producers might contend that, far from being a fault, the way the two acts are divided permits a choreographer to move from everyday reality in the first act to pure fantasy in the second. Having the ballerina do only the *grand pas de deux* helps make the Sugarplum Fairy seem a truly enchanted vision. If she were present throughout the ballet, she might come to seem ordinary. By restricting her to a tantalizingly few appearances, she remains a mysterious creature from another world. Moreover this sense of mystery is intensified by contrasting her with a perfectly ordinary little girl, such as Clara. As for *The Nutcracker*'s alleged sentimentality, that can be defended as an attempt by Petipa to offer a picture of happy family life; *The Nutcracker*, after all, is a Christmas ballet, and Christmas is a time for charm, warmth, and nostalgia, not for grotesque fantasies.

Below
Alexandre Volinine appeared with Anna Pavlova at the Theatre Royal, Drury Lane in 1920 in a ballet called *Snowflakes* which used *Nutcracker* music. They danced together as the Prince and the Snow Queen.

Other producers, however, have considered at least some of the objections to *The Nutcracker* to be valid. These producers, therefore, have tried to come up with ingenious ways to expand the ballerina role. Many have modified the plot, while a few have scrapped the original scenario altogether, preferring new narratives of their own devising. Hence there exist so many versions of *The Nutcracker*. Usually the one thing they have in common is the Tchaikovsky score. Yet odd things have also been done with the music.

Right
The immortal Russian ballerina Anna Pavlova partnered by Nijinsky in a *pas de deux*.

Above
Yekaterina Maximova as
Marie and V Levashov
as the Puppeteer in the
Bolshoi production.
Right
Yekaterina Maximova as
Marie and Vladimir
Vasiliev as the Nut-
cracker Prince in the
Bolshoi Ballet produc-
tion premiered in
Moscow on 12 March
1966.
Above right
N Bessmertnova as
Marie and M Lavrovsky
in the Grigorovich
production.

The Russians themselves were the first to start tinkering with *The Nutcracker*. Their modifications began so soon after the premiere and were sometimes so extensive that over the years most of Ivanov's original choreography has been irretrievably lost. The Russians not only changed *The Nutcracker*, they on occasion combined bits of *The Nutcracker* with other ballets. In 1909 the Ballets Russes of Serge Diaghilev astonished Paris with choreography that was, at the time, considered to be avant-garde. The repertoire also contained a suite of dances to various pieces of music called *Le Festin* which included the *Nutcracker* Trepak with new choreography—but in the traditional style—by Michel Fokine (1880–1942) who, as Diaghilev's most innovative choreographer, usually tackled much more ambitious projects than the staging of *divertissements*. Vaslav Nijinsky (1889–1950), Diaghilev's

leading male dancer, used *The Nutcracker* music for a new solo for himself as the Prince in *Swan Lake* in 1911. Not only does no one remember what that choreography was like, scholars find it difficult even to speculate as to what it could have been like, since the *Nutcracker* music that Nijinsky chose to interpolate for himself was the Sugarplum Fairy's variation, complete with tinkling celesta—music which, by the standards of turn-of-the-century ballet, sounds inescapably feminine in manner. Bits of *The Nutcracker* found their way into yet another Diaghilev production of a Tchaikovsky ballet in 1921 when his company presented the complete *Sleeping Beauty* for the first time in London. To make an already spectacular work seem even more spectacular, choreographer Bronislava Nijinska (1891–1972), sister of Nijinsky, added the Arabian and Chinese Dances from *The Nutcracker* and

had the Lilac Fairy, the symbol of goodness, dance the Sugarplum Fairy's variation.

Until her death in 1931, the Russian ballerina Anna Pavlova toured the world with a ballet company of her own, offering the classics (either in their entirety or in sets of excerpts) and new ballets in the familiar classic style. In 1915 her ballet master Ivan Clustine (1862–1941) choreographed a ballet called *Snowflakes*, a set of whirling dances for winter sprites, to music from *Swan Lake* and *The Nutcracker*. As might be expected the music from *The Nutcracker* was taken from the snow sequence. To one of the melodies, Clustine created a *pas de deux* for Pavlova and Alexandre Volinine as a Snow Queen and her Prince. This *pas de deux* was so successful that, ever since then, choreographers have occasionally introduced a *pas de deux* into the snow scene of *The Nutcracker*, although no such *pas de deux* occurred in Ivanov's original production. Often the female role in the *pas de deux* is danced by the same woman who dances the Sugarplum Fairy—this being one way of giving the ballerina additional things to do. In other productions the Snow Queen

Anna Pavlova, at 15 years (*above right*) and in her dressing room (*below left*). She formed her own ballet company and toured the world.

Below left
Yekaterina Maximova as Marie in the Bolshoi production. Grigorovich made the part of Marie one for an adult dancer.
Below
Natalia Bessmertnova as Marie and Mikhail Lavrovsky as the Nutcracker Prince.

and the Sugarplum Fairy are treated as totally separate roles, each being assigned to a different ballerina. These productions, as a result, permit more than one leading dancer to shine, if only for a few minutes, in *The Nutcracker*.

One of the most famous early Russian revisions of the complete *Nutcracker* was that made by Alexander Gorsky (1871–1924) for the Bolshoi Ballet of Moscow in 1919. Gorsky had once been a pupil of Petipa, but Petipa distrusted him and considered him something of an upstart. While serving as chief choreographer for the Bolshoi, Gorsky came under the influence of Constantin Stanislavsky's Moscow Art Theater which was then revolutionizing acting and stage direction with its devotion to ideals of theatrical truth and believability and its realistic productions of such playwrights as Ibsen and Chekhov. Gorsky tried to introduce comparable principles of realism into ballet with results that are still controversial. Few of Gorsky's ballets are totally original, most of them being his personal adaptations of existing works by Petipa. Gorsky believed that many of Petipa's symmetrical choreographic groupings were unduly artificial and broke them up with asymmetrical designs. He also introduced realistic touches of stage business. A dynamic company director, Gorsky revitalized the Bolshoi Ballet, which before his arrival had been considered provincial. Nevertheless ballet historians still debate the wisdom and validity of his reinterpretations of Petipa.

In accordance with his concern for realism, Gorsky made the first act of *The Nutcracker* a very realistic depiction of a nineteenth-century bourgeois home. The rest of the ballet, the little girl's dream, began with the musing child tracing designs with her fingers on a frosted windowpane, the designs on the pane giving way to the dance of the snowflakes. Coming only a few years after the Bolshevik Revolution, this version of *The Nutcracker* was produced at a time of economic deprivation in Russia when some materials were scarce or even non-existent. The wardrobe departments of ballet companies suffered because there was no tarlatan

available to make tutus. Konstantin Korovine, Gorsky's designer, circumvented this problem by dispensing with tutus, even though they were the traditional costumes for the snowflakes. Instead he dressed his snowflakes in fabrics which in texture and appearance simulated Russian fur coats and had the dancers hold their hands in muffs. Gorsky's production also implied that the Sugarplum Fairy was Clara's idealized vision of the beautiful adult woman she would like to grow up to be. Gorsky here initiated a tendency, which continues to this day, for producers of *The Nutcracker* to relate Clara and the Sugarplum Fairy in some psychologically significant fashion.

Russian art of the 1920s was freewheeling and often daringly experimental. Russian ballet was often equally unconventional. Whereas some of the innovations were profound in their implications, others seem like high-spirited larks by choreographers intoxicated by the idea of modernity. It was this heady period which gave birth to a choreographically peculiar *Nutcracker* by Fyodor Lopukhov (1886–1973) in which the settings were flat panels carried on and off stage by the dancers themselves. The ballerina and her partner began their their *grand pas de deux* by turning cartwheels and at one point in the *pas de deux* the ballerina was lifted head downwards while doing the splits. This *Nutcracker* confirmed Lopukhov's reputation as a brilliant, if sometimes eccentric, choreographer.

Left
Nina Sorokina as Masha and Yuri Vladimirov as the Nutcracker Prince in the 1966 Bolshoi production.
Right
Nina Sorokina as the Princess and Vladimir Nikonov as the Nutcracker Prince in a debut performance at the Kremlin Palace of Congresses given in June 1963.

A Soviet production that proved more influential not only in Russia but, indirectly, nen (1901-1964) for the Leningrad Kirov Ballet in 1934. It was Vainonen who found a way for *The Nutcracker* to contain a challenging ballerina role that extended over both acts. Instead of making his first-act heroine a seven-year-old, he turned Masha (as his Clara was named) into an adolescent, which meant that the part could be performed by an adult dancer. In the first act Masha is presented with a ballerina doll, a jack-in-the-box, and a golliwog doll. She decides that the golliwog is her favorite Christmas gift, and it is he who saves her from the mice, after which he turns into a handsome prince, the same prince with whom she dances the *pas de deux* customarily assigned to the Sugarplum Fairy and her Prince. Two great Russian ballerinas became celebrated for their interpretation of Masha:

Galina Ulanova, at the premiere, and in a revival several seasons later, Maya Pliset-skaya. Developing certain implications of the Gorsky production, the Vainonen rendering of *The Nutcracker* is an important early attempt to make Clara and the Sugarplum Fairy essentially the same person. Other productions by other choreographers have continued to make the same identification. The Vainonen version is also one in which, despite the title, a nutcracker is of little or no importance. There will be others of this kind as well.

The latest Russian development of the approach to *The Nutcracker* exemplified by the Vainonen is the production by Yuri Grigorovich (1927–) premiered in Moscow by the Bolshoi Ballet on 12 March 1966, starring Yekaterina Maximova and Vladimir Vasiliev. In this version Marie, the little girl of the first act, becomes an idealized fairy-tale princess in the second and is about to marry the Nutcracker Prince when she wakes up and discovers that all her adventures have been only a dream. So conceived, the role of Marie (like Vainonen's Masha) is a part for an adult ballerina. Grigorovich gives the leading male dancer who portrays the Nutcracker an equally complex role, for the Nutcracker is successively transformed from a grotesque mannikin into a magical warrior and, finally, into a handsome prince. Siding with those who feel that the conventional scenario for *The Nutcracker* is dramatically tepid, Grigorovich has tried to find ways to intensify the impact of the narrative.

The plot unfolds in a storybook manner with the party guests slightly caricatured, as though these adults were seen through the wide and wondering eyes of a curious child. Grigorovich also attempts to make Marie's dream in some way reflect events that have taken place while she was awake. Thus mischievous boys at the party don mouse masks and try to frighten Marie—which presumably helps explain why she has a nightmare populated by mice. To insure that the last half of the ballet is more than a *divertissement*, Grigorovich has the decisive battle with the mice take place in the second rather than the first act, and when the *divertissements* do occur, they are performed by the dolls that have been seen as toys placed under the Christmas tree in the first act. Some critics, however, have found these *divertissements* excessively cute—particularly the dance for the *mirlitons* which Grigorovich has transformed into a pastoral for a shepherd and shepherdess accompanied by a toy lamb on wheels. Other objections have been directed toward the *pas de deux*, which here is no longer really a *pas de deux*, since Grigorovich introduces a background ensemble of men bearing candelabra who pose behind ballerina and *danseur* and at times hold them aloft. Nevertheless despite any weakness of which it may be accused, the Grigorovich *Nutcracker* has been hailed as a version which, while adhering to the familiar story, manages to heighten the dramatic values of that story without becoming freakishly idiosyncratic.

The Nutcracker began to enter the repertoires of Western European companies during the 1930s. One of the first on the Continent was a production by the Ballets de Monte Carlo choreographed by the Russian-born choreographer Boris Romanov (1891–1957). Programs indicated that the décor was by someone named Alexeieff, but whereas Romanov was authentically Russian, the mysterious Alexeieff was fictitious, being only a pseudonym for the British stage designer William Chappell. Romanov made no attempt to reproduce Ivanov's choreography, the dances being entirely his own invention. They were rather odd, too. Perhaps inspired by Pavlova and Clustine, who had used *The Nutcracker* music for a Snow Queen and Prince in *Snowflakes*, Romanov introduced a Snow Queen into *The Nutcracker*'s snow scene. He also made the character *divertissements* of the last act entirely classical in their basic style—or, perhaps, neoclassical might be a better word for them since, although the production's stars were two pure classicists, Vera Nemchinova and Anatole Oboukhoff, Romanov's choreography distorted the line of traditional classicism. The British critic Arnold L Haskell chided Romanov for trying to fit to Tchaikovsky's melodious music 'a jerky, ultramodern production.' This version, said Haskell, constituted 'a vivid lesson in leaving the classics well alone.'

Following that 1936 *Nutcracker* there was one in 1937 at the Paris Opéra-Comique choreographed by Jean-Jacques Etchevery, and in 1938 one at La Scala, Milan, choreographed by Margarita Frohman. What made this production of special interest is that it was conceived and designed by Alexandre Benois who, in the years following his disappointment over the ballet's premiere, had changed his mind about *The Nutcracker*. Now he regarded *The Nutcracker* as an admirable evocation of youthful fantasies and attempted to make his Milanese staging childlike in nature. It adhered, by and large,

Right
Drosselmeyer brings four clockwork dolls to the Christmas party: a Vivandière, a Soldier, a Columbine and a Harlequin danced by Nadina Newhouse, Freda Barnford, Sheila McCarthy and Elizabeth Miller in the 1934 Vic-Wells Ballet revival designed by Hedley Briggs.
Below
Claude Newman as the Buffoon in the same production.

to the traditional scenario, but Benois did try to inject some narrative continuity into the second act by having Drosselmeyer return as the King of the Land of Sweets. In 1956 La Scala produced a totally new *Nutcracker* choreographed by Alfred Rodrigues and designed by James Bailey, with Margot Fonteyn and Michael Somes as guest stars.

Although the Royal Danish Ballet is one of the oldest ballet companies in the world, Denmark did not have a complete *Nutcracker* until Flemming Flindt (1936–) staged it for the company on 11 December 1971, with a cast including Dinna Bjørn (Clara), Mette Hønningen and Henning Kronstam (Nutcracker Princess and Prince), Niels Bjørn Larsen (Drosselmeyer), and Vivi Flindt (Snow Queen). When John Percival of the London *Times* arrived in Copenhagen to take a look at it, Flemming Flindt warned him, 'It's for Danish children, not English critics.' Percival enjoyed it anyway. Flindt employed students from the Royal Danish Ballet School in all the children's roles save

that of Clara, which was given to a small, but adult, dancer. The production, enormously popular in Copenhagen, was traditional in atmosphere, Flindt's only unusual touch being his transformation of the Mirlitons' Dance into one of those curious Russian folk dances from Georgia in which women, wearing long skirts that hide their feet, give the illusion that they are moving smoothly along, as though on casters.

The British *Nutcracker* tradition dates from the 1930s. The first important staging was that of the Vic-Wells Ballet on 30 January 1934, designed by Hedley Briggs. The Vic-Wells was the remarkable company formed by Ninette de Valois which performed alternately at the Old Vic and Sadler's Wells Theatres. Later when it made Sadler's Wells its sole home, its name was changed to the Sadler's Wells Ballet and, still later, in 1956, in recognition of its great contributions to contemporary ballet, it received a Royal Charter and became Britain's Royal Ballet. In charge of the 1934 production was

Above
Alicia Markova and Stanley Judson as the Sugarplum Fairy and her cavalier in the same production.
Right
Alicia Markova as the Sugarplum Fairy and Stanley Judson as her cavalier were featured in the premiere of the 1934 Vic-Wells Ballet production.

the Russian teacher and coach, Nicholas Sergueeff (1876-1951), a dry, pedantic man who, if dancers who worked with him are to be trusted, possessed little theatrical flair of his own. He was, however, blessed with an extraordinary knowledge of the Russian classics, due both to his own memory and to the fact that he had taken out of Russia with him a collection of notated scores of ballets in the Stepanov system of dance notation. Sergueeff claimed that his Vic-Wells production consisted of the choreography he had known at the Maryinsky adapted to the special requirements of a small company. The premiere of the Vic-Wells version starred Alicia Markova and Stanley Judson as the Sugarplum Fairy and her Prince. Later that season Ruth French also danced the Fairy, and both Anton Dolin and Harold Turner were seen as the Prince.

The regular Vic-Wells ensemble was augmented for *The Nutcracker* by child actors from the Lord Mayor's Boy Players, who

Above
Mary Honer and Robert Helpmann in 1937.

appeared as toy soldiers and mice. Another addition to the cast was actress Elsa Lanchester, who was cast in the Arabian *divertissement*. Sergueeff had watched Lanchester rehearse as Ariel in Shakespeare's *The Tempest* at the Old Vic. After deciding that he wanted to use her in *The Nutcracker*, he rushed into the Old Vic office, gesticulating wildly and screaming, 'Dramateek lady! Dramateek lady!' until the startled management was able to make out that he was referring to Elsa Lanchester.

The Nutcracker was remounted by the Vic-Wells on 8 January 1937 with new décor and costumes by Mstislav Doboujinsky. On this occasion the stars were Margot Fonteyn and Robert Helpmann. In 1934 Helpmann had appeared in the Chinese Dance, while Fonteyn had made her stage début, under the name of Peggy Hookham on 21 April 1934 as a snowflake in *The Nutcracker*. Now audiences were beginning to recognize them as two of the greatest talents in British ballet and their partnership became a famous one.

Sergueeff's *Nutcracker* was usually presented in its entirety, but on some occasions only the second act was offered. In 1946 the main Sadler's Wells Ballet moved into the Royal Opera House, Covent Garden, and a second company under the same management—a 'junior' company specializing in

Above
Robert Helpmann in
1948.
Right
Mary Honer as the
Sugarplum Fairy and
Robert Helpmann as her
cavalier in the revival of
The Nutcracker first
presented at the Sadler's
Wells Theatre on
8 January 1937.
Far right
Alicia Markova and
Anton Dolin in the
London Festival Ballet's
first production of *The
Nutcracker*, staged by
Nicholas Beriozoff and
premiered on 24 October
1950.
Below
Margot Fonteyn in 1937.
She made her debut in
the 1934 Vic-Wells
production as a
snowflake.

the training and development of young dancers—was established at Sadler's Wells. This company, the Sadler's Wells Theatre Ballet, inherited the second act of the Sergueeff version, dancing it for the first time on 8 April 1946, with Margaret Dale and Norman Thomson in the *pas de deux*.

Although *The Nutcracker* seemed reasonably popular with the general public, London critics—like their St Petersburg counterparts of 1892—tended to sniff at the ballet with slight disdain. Cyril W Beaumont, dean of English ballet historians, declared, 'The opening scene possesses little of interest save a pleasant old-world charm, for the dances by the dolls and the fight between the soldiers and the mice are frankly undistinguished and only suited to a juvenile audience.' However, he pronounced the Dance of the Snowflakes (who, as in 1892, carried branched sticks topped with fleecy balls of snow) 'a charming spectacle,' but found little rhyme or reason in the second act *divertissements*. Calling the choreography for them 'seldom appropriate to the situation' and 'of indifferent quality,' he admitted that he could not understand why coffee was represented by a Mideastern 'stomach dance' and tea by some Chinamen out of 'a pantomime version of Aladdin.' Best of all for Beaumont was the *grand pas de deux* which he considered of genuine merit.

Still audiences did want to see *The Nutcracker*, and when Alicia Markova and Anton Dolin headed a touring company of their

Below
The snowflakes from the 1937 Vic-Wells production with scenery and costumes by Mstislav Doboujinsky. Clara and her prince pass through the Fir Forest in winter on their way to the Land of Sweets.

own from 1935 to 1938, excerpts from the second act figured in the repertoire of the Markova-Dolin Ballet. Another English company, Ballet Rambert, included the second act (designed by Harry Cordwell) in the repertoire of its 1948 tour of Australia. An unusual single-act version of *The Nutcracker* was that choreographed by Frederick Ashton (1904–) and designed by Cecil Beaton which superseded the Sergueeff staging in the repertoire of the Sadler's Wells Theatre Ballet. Ashton's new interpretation was premiered 11 September 1951. Apparently taking to heart the complaints that the first-act story was uninteresting, Ashton dispensed with story entirely, making the ballet a plotless fantasy that included the snowflake scene and the second act festivities. Although the dances were based upon the Ivanov style, only parts of the *pas de deux* and the Chinese

Above
David Blair and Elaine Fifield in the 1949 revival of the production staged by the Sadler's Wells Theatre Ballet in 1946.

Dance were left unchanged, Ashton re-choreographing the rest of the ballet. The *pas de deux* (for Elaine Fifield and David Blair) included a new male variation for Blair which began with two double turns in the air in quick succession, then considered a virtuoso feat in British male dancing. There was also a *pas de deux* for a Snow Queen and a Snow King (Svetlana Beriosova and Robert Lunnon). Maryon Lane led the Waltz of the Flowers. Freed of narrative, Ashton's *Nutcracker* offered such an array of choreographic sweets that *The Dancing Times* characterized it as 'a rich, almost indigestible spectacle relieved only by passages of magnificently austere classical dance. . . .'

The year before Ashton choreographed his *Nutcracker*, London Festival Ballet offered what would prove to be the first of several *Nutcracker* productions. This one,

staged by Nicholas Beriozoff (1906–) and designed by George Kirsta, starred Alicia Markova and Anton Dolin at the premiere on 24 October 1950. During the next few seasons several choreographers modified Beriozoff's choreography for one dance or another, the tinkerers including Markova and Dolin themselves, David Lichine, Grace Cone, and Pilar Lopez. Finally, on 24 December 1957, Festival Ballet staged an entirely new *Nutcracker*—possibly the most famous of all its *Nutcracker*s—choreographed by David Lichine (1910–1972), who had set the Waltz of the Flowers and the Snowflake scene in one of the revisions of the 1950 version. He had also choreographed a *Nutcracker* for the Borovansky Ballet in Australia. What made the 1957 *Nutcracker* particularly important was that it had designs by the old master, Alexandre Benois.

In his research on the ballet, Lichine consulted with three retired Russian ballerinas, Mathilde Kschessinska, Lubov Egorova, and Olga Preobrajenska about early Maryinsky performances in which they had danced, and discovered to his amazement that each had entirely different recollections of the work. Invaluable help came from Benois, who told Lichine what he remembered of the original production and made suggestions about details of choreography and dramatic action. He might have made even more extensive suggestions if it had not been for his age. A venerable, benign sage of 87, he lived quietly in Paris, unable to get about easily, but always making sure that his numerous pet cats were well fed.

Except for Beriozoff's Trepak, which was retained from the earlier staging, and the traditional 'after Ivanov' *pas de deux* (reproduced by Anton Dolin), the 1957 choreography was entirely the work of Lichine. The cast included Nathalie Krassovska and John Gilpin as Sugarplum Fairy and Prince, and Dolin as Drosselmeyer. Children's roles were taken by students from the Arts Educational Schools. The choreography for the children was almost universally admired, Lichine having been able to make his young dancers look lively and charming, but never obstreperous or coy. Only one detail in the children's scenes received adverse criticism. When Clara arrived in the Land of Sweets, little cooks presented her with a gigantic lollipop. After consuming too much of it she came down with a tummy ache. That, said the reviewers, was an excessively naturalistic touch, especially since the ballet was set in a magic candy kingdom where, presumably, tummy aches did not exist.

Most critics tended to agree with Clive Barnes that 'Lichine's choreography, if not very original,' possessed the virtue 'of never being obtrusive. For a man usually so prodigal of invention, his work—especially for the children—is a model of almost austere discretion.' Mary Clarke particularly liked the party scene, but thought that Lichine's powers of invention tended to flag in the *divertissements*. The Lichine production was largely straightforward and conventional, differing from similar treatments of the scenario only in detail. Most noticeably, unlike many productions, his Drosselmeyer did not have a charming nephew. Therefore when the nutcracker was transformed into a handsome prince, he became, not Clara's idealization of young Drosselmeyer, but the Sugarplum Fairy's cavalier. The *divertissement* began with a Spanish dance for a cast of ten. The Arabian dance (Coffee) was a duet for a languid Near Eastern couple, the man drinking coffee as he danced, balancing the cup upon the sole of his partner's upraised foot. In Tea two ladies danced with a Chinese mandarin who made his entrance by popping out of a teapot. The Mirlitons were three marzipan shepherdesses, and three Russian dolls bounded through the Trepak. For the first time in British ballet, Mère Gigogne, here called 'Madame Regnier, a bonbonnière,' appeared with her brood. After these *divertissements* came the Waltz of the Flowers, *pas de deux*, and finale.

Perhaps because its very popularity made it so often performed, the Lichine *Nutcracker* began to grow bedraggled over the years until 1965 when Norman McDowell, then Artistic Director of Festival Ballet, sought to refurbish it. Philip Prowse (who would later design a *Nutcracker* for Scottish Ballet) took some of the wrinkles and creases out of

the Benois designs, and McDowell consulted the esteemed Russian ballerina Tamara Karsavina, who relayed her suggestions to a team of choreographers including Andrée Howard, Alexander Ursuliak, Vassilie Trunoff, and Jack Carter. McDowell countenanced several innovations. He made a tentative experiment involving costuming the nutcracker doll to look something like a contemporary spaceman; but since the nutcracker thereby looked anachronistic amidst the cosy Victorianism of the rest of the production, this modification of costuming was soon abandoned. A *pas de deux* for a Snow Queen and a Snow Prince (for which there was no equivalent in the Lichine) was added, and the Sugarplum Fairy's role in the second act was expanded with the addition of a new dance for the ballerina and four male partners during which she was thrown from one man to another and finally caught in what ballet students have nicknamed a 'fish dive.' Since most *Nutcrackers* end with Clara leaving the Land of Sweets, they imply that she will awake from her Christmas dream, yet few actually present the awakening. McDowell did so by showing Clara being found by her parents at the foot of the family Christmas tree, still clutching her nutcracker doll. When Beryl Grey became artistic director of Festival Ballet in 1968, this composite Benois–Lichine–McDowell *Nutcracker* by committee remained in the repertoire until 1976, when it gave way to a Ronald Hynd version which will be discussed further in the section on 'eccentric' *Nutcrackers*.

After Festival Ballet the next English company to attempt *The Nutcracker* was Walter Gore's short-lived London Ballet, which unveiled its *Nutcracker*, choreographed by Gore (1910–   ) after Ivanov, on 4 October 1962 at the Brighton Pavilion with Gore's wife Paula Hinton as the Sugarplum Fairy, Alexis Rassine as her Prince, Barrie Wilkinson as the Nutcracker Prince, Jane Rowland Evans as Clara, and Gore as Drosselmeyer. The designs were by Harry Cordwell, who had designed the 1948 Ballet Rambert version. In terms of dramatic action this 1962 version was based upon a *Nutcracker* Gore had staged in Holland in 1959.

Above
Rudolf Nureyev in his production for the Royal Ballet in 1968.
Above right
Alicia Markova with Anton Dolin at the Haringay Arena, London.
Far right
Nathalie Krassovska and Boris Trailine as the Sugarplum Fairy and her prince in the 1948 Ballet Rambert Tour of Australia.
Right
The Arab Dance from the London Festival Ballet production by David Lichine.

Rudolf Nureyev as The Prince
and Antoinette Sibley as The
Princess in a production by
the Royal Ballet.
Inset right
David Blair and Elaine Fifield
in the 1949 Sadler's Wells
Theatre Ballet production.
Inset below
Doreen Wells and Patrice Bart
(London Festival Ballet).

The battle of the toys and the mice was omitted, Clara falling asleep after the party and in her dreams journeying immediately to the land of enchantment (a treatment of the scenario remarkably similar to that which the Ballet Russe de Monte Carlo toured across America in the 1940s and 1950s). Thus condensed, the scenes in *The Nutcracker* could be played through continuously without the need of a formal interval. Gore's *Nutcracker* was a long one-act, rather than a full-evening, ballet which did not attempt the scenic splendor of more ambitious productions. It also did not have the impact of such productions and there were critics, among them Clive Barnes, who complained that Gore excessively burlesqued the characterizations of the adult guests at the Christmas party.

Whatever form it might have taken, British audiences grew increasingly fond of *The Nutcracker*. Rudolf Nureyev staged his 'eccentric' version for the Royal Ballet in 1968, the first *Nutcracker* the Royal Ballet organization had sponsored since Ashton's 1951 production for the Sadler's Wells Theatre Ballet. Although it is not a permanent part of the Royal Ballet repertoire, the Nureyev *Nutcracker* is frequently revived. One revival occurred in 1976 which, for British balletgoers, was a bumper year for *Nutcracker*s, since that year one had, in addition to the Nureyev version, three other *Nutcracker*s from which to choose: Ronald Hynd's for Festival Ballet, Peter Darrell's for Scottish Ballet, and Ben Stevenson's for Ballet International, a company which lasted for only one season despite the fact that it had ambitious plans and a roster of talented dancers. Ballet International's *Nutcracker*, first shown in England on 6 December 1976 in Bournemouth, proceeded along traditional lines, Stevenson's major quirk being that of making the Stahlbaums a somewhat rustic family, not the prosperous burghers they usually appear to be. Among Stevenson's personal touches in the *divertissements* were an Arabian dance for two dancers and a coffee pot and the use of the Mère Gigogne music for a Punch and Judy show.

Darrell's Scottish production, designed by Philip Prowse, was first seen in its entirety in Edinburgh on 19 December 1973, with Anna-Marie Holmes as the Sugarplum Fairy, Michael Beare as the Prince, and Marian St Claire as the Snow Queen. The previous year, on 26 September 1972, in York the company had presented the second act of *The Nutcracker* as its first installment in what would eventually become a complete production. Typical of how *The Nutcracker* affects the box office was the fact that the Edinburgh Christmas season of 1973 had a record advance sale.

As conceived by Darrell, Drosselmeyer was very much a magician. He entered with three assistants, who later became the Snow Queen, Sugarplum Fairy, and Nutcracker Prince in Clara's dream. The vocalists in the snow scene, who are usually confined to the wings or the orchestra pit were brought on stage by Darrell, garbed as carol singers. A moment in the first act that mystified some critics was actually a little joke on Darrell's part. At the end of the Christmas party, everyone left dressed for the outdoors. Why, wondered the critics, did the party's host and hostess appear to be leaving their own house? Where were they going? Darrell later confessed that he imagined all these people hurrying away to attend a performance of *The Nutcracker* at the local playhouse! But this, of course, had to remain a private joke known only to Darrell and his friends, since there was really no way that this explanation could be made on stage in terms of mime.

North America

Despite the popularity of *The Nutcracker* in other countries, the ballet's true home is the United States where, each Christmas, it is produced by scores of companies, big and small, professional and amateur, in cities, towns, and villages from coast to coast. Americans, so it would seem, cannot get enough of *The Nutcracker*, nor are they content to see it only at Christmas. *The Nut-cracker* appears to be welcome at any time of the year. One of the newest major productions, that of Mikhail Baryshnikov for American Ballet Theater, was first shown to New Yorkers in the spring of 1977 and made its next appearance in Manhattan the following September. During the 1950s the New York City Ballet occasionally brought its *Nutcracker* to Chicago in the springtime, and for two decades after its premiere in 1940 the Ballet Russe de Monte Carlo constantly took *The Nutcracker* up and down the American continent throughout the year.

Marianna Tcherkassky as Clara and Mikhail Baryshnikov as the Nutcracker Prince in the production choreographed by Baryshnikov for the American Ballet Theater.

If any company started the vogue for *The Nutcracker* in the United States, it was the Ballet Russe de Monte Carlo. Consisting in its early days largely of Russian dancers or dancers of Russian emigré parents, the Ballet Russe was a cosmopolitan company which before World War II regularly toured both Europe and America. Domiciled in the United States for the duration of the war, it increasingly became an American company in all but its fancy exotic name. Staged 'after Ivanov' by Alexandra Fedorova (1884–1972), *The Nutcracker* was first presented by the Ballet Russe on 17 October 1940 at New York City's 51st Street Theater, starring Alicia Markova and André Eglevsky (who, to expand their roles, appeared in both the Snow and the Sugarplum Fairy scenes). Although the designs were by Alexander Benois, he was unable to supervise their realization in America. Living in German-occupied Paris, Benois entrusted his sketches for scenery and costumes to a friend who, because of the disruption of the French transportation system at the time, walked with them all the way to Lyon, where they were

Michele Abraham as the little girl, who is called Marie, and members of the Minnesota Dance Theater in the production choreographed by Loyce Houlton.

given to another friend who superintended their delivery to the Ballet Russe in America. They almost never made it, however, for they were impounded by customs and immigration authorities who had to be convinced that these drawings of fairies, dolls, and truculent mice were not in reality coded messages having something to do with espionage and the war effort.

The Ballet Russe *Nutcracker* was performed without intermission as a single, long, one-act ballet that proceeded from the Christmas party to Clara's dream of the realms of the Snow Queen and the Sugarplum Fairy. Although Benois designed costume sketches for the battle with the mice, that scene was omitted. Other episodes were also discreetly trimmed. The party scene in particular was reduced to the barest essentials that would make the plot comprehensible. Because of the abridgments, this *Nutcracker* could fit on a program with as many as two other works, and a triple-bill consisting of the second act of the Petipa-Ivanov *Swan Lake*, *The Nutcracker*, and Michel Fokine's *Scheherazade* became one of the most popular and frequently danced programs of the Ballet Russe.

To facilitate touring, children's parts were played by adult dancers who happened to be short of stature. The role of Clara in one scene was sometimes an exception, however. Although Clara was always played by an adult in the party episode, sometimes an actual child was used for the second act entrance into the Kingdom of Sweets. The Ballet Russe discovered that this practice could be good publicity. In some cities on tour, contests were held to pick the child for that night's performance. In other cities the daughter of some prominent local citizen— the mayor or a leading businessman or educator—would be chosen as Clara. At one Hollywood performance, the Clara was Maureen Reagan, daughter of screen stars Ronald Reagan and Jane Wyman.

As the years passed, constant touring caused the Ballet Russe *Nutcracker* to grow shabby. This staging was surely one of those to which music and dance critic Robert Lawrence alluded in 1950 when he observed that

'In the drabness of certain current productions of *The Nutcracker*, seasonal festivities at a Bowery mission are suggested.' Always an abridgment from the very start, the Ballet Russe *Nutcracker* was steadily cut over the course of time until P W Manchester could complain in 1954 that 'This company's version of *The Nutcracker* is . . . an extremely poor one, with the whole of the first scene compressed into about five perfunctory minutes which reduces even this tenuous story to complete incomprehensibility.' Eventually the first scene was omitted entirely. The snowflake scene was also dropped, reducing the production to the second act *divertissements*. The Ballet Russe *Nutcracker* may have deteriorated to a shocking degree, but it was the first *Nutcracker* many Americans ever saw, and it did much to encourage the American *Nutcracker* mania.

The first complete American *Nutcracker* was that of William Christensen (1902-) for the San Francisco Ballet in 1944. The production came about because the San Francisco War Memorial Opera House,

Below
The Company of the Royal Winnipeg Ballet in the production choreographed by John Neumeier and designed by Jurgen Rose. Neumeier changed the original story and made his heroine a 12-year-old girl named Maria and made the setting her birthday party.

Above
David Voss as Drossel-
meyer in the Loyce
Houlton production for
the Minnesota Dance
Theater.
Above right
Salvatore Aiello as
Drosselmeyer in John
Neumeier's production
for the Royal Winnipeg
Ballet. In this version
Drosselmeyer is cast as
an eccentric ballet
master who brings Maria
(Clara) a pair of point
shoes for her birthday.

which the ballet company shared with the
local symphony orchestra and opera company, was almost always vacant at Christmas.
Previously the San Francisco Ballet had
danced a *Hansel and Gretel* ballet during the
holiday season. San Francisco possessed a
colony of ardent White Russian balletomanes, and some of them suggested to
Christensen that he stage *The Nutcracker*,
even though he protested that he had never
even seen a complete production of the ballet
before. Nevertheless he was interested in
the classics—he had choreographed the
first full-length American productions of
Coppélia and *Swan Lake*—and he started
examining the score for *The Nutcracker* and
discussing the ballet with persons who had
seen it in the past. Particularly fruitful was a
conversation with Alexandra Danilova (ballerina of the Ballet Russe de Monte Carlo
and herself an acclaimed Sugarplum Fairy)
and the choreographer George Balanchine.
They talked long into the night, Balanchine
growing increasingly enthusiastic about the
project, this discussion perhaps being the

Patricia McBride and
Edward Villella as the
Sugarplum Fairy and
her cavalier in a New
York City Ballet
production.
Right
The children of the New
York City Ballet Com-
pany in the production
choreographed by
George Balanchine.

seed out of which would grow a new Balanchine production of *The Nutcracker* a decade later. Danilova often demonstrated steps from Russian productions with which she was familiar, but Balanchine always cautioned, 'Let him do his own choreography.'

With scenery by Antonio Sotomayer and costumes by San Francisco designer, critic, and dance historian Russell Hartley, the San Francisco Ballet premiered its *Nutcracker* on 29 December 1944. Gisella Caccialanza was the Sugarplum Fairy and Christensen was her cavalier. The Christensen family is one of the great families of American dance. William's brother Harold is a notable teacher who has headed the faculty of the San Francisco Ballet School; ballerina Gisella Caccialanza is married to yet another Christensen brother, the dancer and choreographer Lew Christensen, who eventually succeeded William as director of the San Francisco Ballet when William went to Salt Lake City in 1951 to establish the company Ballet West.

It was Lew Christensen (1909–) who choreographed the next San Francisco Ballet

Nutcracker which had its first performance on 18 December 1954, with Nancy Johnson and Conrad Ludlow as the Sugarplum Fairy and Prince, and Sally Bailey and Gordon Paxman leading the snowflakes. This production, designed by Leonard Weisgard, was repeated each Christmas and became enormously popular. In the thirteen years after its premiere, it was seen by more than 400,000 people. Lew Christensen's decision to make this *Nutcracker* as childlike as possible is reflected in the type of choreography he provided for the various scenes. The dancing dolls that Drosselmeyer presented as Christmas gifts in the first act included a ballerina doll partnered by a huge brown furry bear—always a great favorite of young audiences. The second act *divertissements* resembled illustrations from children's storybooks come alive. In the Spanish Dance three chocolate Spanish bullfighters appeared with a licorice bull. A Turkish magician made a dancing girl disappear during the Arabian Dance. The Chinese Dance featured a tea peddler. The Mirlitons'

Above
Scene from the party as staged by the American Ballet Theater.
Right
In the Ballet West version of *The Nutcracker* the two mechanical dolls which Drosselmeyer presents are a ballerina and a life-size brown bear.

In the Hynd production for the London Festival Ballet Fritz appears in Clara's dream as the commander of a ship crossing the Lemonade Sea to the Kingdom of Sweets.

115

Clara examines the life-size dolls which Drossel-meyer has brought to the Christmas party (Minnesota Dance Theater).

Left
Drosselmeyer presents Clara with a hand-carved nutcracker (San Jose Dance Theater).
Right
Alain Dubreuil and Patricia Ruanne in the *grand pas de deux* from Act II of the London Festival Ballet production.

The magic comes to an end as Clara's parents find her asleep by the Christmas tree and Drosselmeyer vanishes in the shadows (San Jose Dance Theater).

music accompanied a number for candybox shepherdesses and two little lambs. The Trepak became a ribbon candy dance. Mère Gigogne (renamed Mother Marshmallow) made her entrance, after which came the Waltz of the Flowers, the *grand pas de deux*, and the finale (during which Clara and the Nutcracker Prince sailed home in a balloon).

When, in the course of time, the décor started to show signs of age, Christensen renewed his *Nutcracker* production. In 1967 it acquired fresh designs by Robert O'Hearn, and Christensen also revised his choreography. The Arabian Dance was again a magic act and ribbon candy still leaped through the Trepak, and Mother Marshmallow, the Waltz of the Flowers, and the *grand pas de deux* were retained. The Spanish *divertissement* became a dance for three couples, a man battled a paper dragon during the Chinese Dance, and wood nymphs cavorted to the Mirlitons. Conrad Ludlow, now of the New York City Ballet, returned to the San Francisco Ballet that year to dance the role of the Nutcracker Prince which he had created in 1954, and two other New York City Ballet stars, Melissa Hayden and Jacques d'Amboise, also appeared as guest artists at certain performances that season.

The most famous and probably the most influential of all American *Nutcracker*s is that choreographed by George Balanchine (1904–   ) for the New York City Ballet. It was premiered at the New York City Center for Music and Drama on 2 February 1954, with Maria Tallchief and Nicholas Magallanes in the *grand pas de deux*, Tanaquil Le Clercq as the Dewdrop who sparkles in the Waltz of the Flowers, and Alberta Grant and Paul Nickel (heading a special cast of children from the School of American Ballet) as Clara and the little Nutcracker Prince. The Drosselmeyer was Michael Arshansky, ordinarily the company's makeup artist. In his native Russia he had begun his career as an actor with the Moscow Art Theater, and now he was able to reveal to American audiences his fine dramatic presence without having to contend with a language barrier. Also in that first cast, among the children who portray the little angels who welcome

Clara and the Nutcracker Prince to Candyland, was Martha Swope, then a ballet student, but today one of the world's best known dance photographers. Horace Armistead designed the scenery, while Karinska was responsible for the costumes, and the lighting was the work of Jean Rosenthal, at that time the company's resident lighting designer.

As a pupil of the Imperial Ballet School in St Petersburg, Balanchine had danced at various times in the Maryinsky *Nutcracker*, his roles ranging in terms of virtue, villainy, and virtuosity from the child Prince to the Mouse King to the Trepak. In his own *Nutcracker* he retained what he remembered of the Maryinsky choreography for the little Prince's mime scene and the Trepak. For the rest of the ballet, as critic Edwin Denby put it, Balanchine used the old classical vocabulary in a new way, selecting 'steps and figures of Ivanov's time, one might like to say steps that Tchaikovsky had seen. Balanchine's dancers like to use their fine speed and sharpness, their rhythmic flexibility and musical ear; so he gave them the old steps with swifter displacements, in rhythms that are fresh, or in new virtuoso combinations.'

Relishing mimetic as well as purely dance effects, Balanchine offers a finely detailed party scene. Several spectacular scenic transformations occur as part of Clara's dream and there is a vivid battle with the mice. Balanchine's Dance of the Snowflakes has been much admired, although he is one of the choreographers who elects not to have a separate *pas de deux* for a Snow Queen and her consort. In 1954 the second act *divertissements* begin with a Spanish dance for two soloists and a supporting ensemble. The Arabian Dance was a solo for a languid Arabian gentleman who, observed by four tiny parrots (played by children), sat on a rug, drinking coffee and smoking a hookah, never exerting himself very much, no matter what he did, and finally falling asleep. A Chinese boy emerged from a lacquered box in the Chinese Dance, jumped about like an Oriental jumping-jack—even doing splits in the air—and then popped back into the box which was rolled off stage by two lady

Patricia McBride and
Jean-Pierre Bonnefous
in the popular New
York City Ballet pro-
duction choreographed
by George Balanchine.

attendants. The Trepak was the brilliant and difficult dance with a hoop Balanchine remembered from the Maryinsky. Dainty marzipan shepherdesses appeared in the Mirlitons' *divertissement*. The New York City Ballet turned Mère Gigogne into Mother Ginger, thereby fracturing her original French name. Whatever her name, she and the children concealed beneath her hoop skirt always win applause. Although Balanchine declined to include a Snow Queen, he did give his *Nutcracker* a secondary ballerina role by having the Waltz of the Flowers led by a Dewdrop. To some balletgoers' disappointment, Balanchine also declined to use what is remembered of Ivanov's choreography for the *grand pas de deux*, inventing new steps of his own instead. He further disappointed certain balletgoers by dispensing with the traditional structure of the classic *pas de deux*. The male dancer receives no solo variation, while the Sugarplum Fairy performs her variation at what is virtually the beginning of the second act. The resultant *pas de deux* consists merely of adagio and

coda. Nevertheless these grounds for complaint are minor. As a whole the Balanchine *Nutcracker* is, by nearly universal assent, a grand balletic spectacle for the holidays.

When the New York City Ballet moved into the New York State Theater of Lincoln Center in 1964, it was discovered that the Horace Armistead designs were too small for the big space in which the company was now performing, and new scenery was commissioned from Rouben Ter-Arutunian. At various times in the history of the New York City Ballet *Nutcracker*, there have also been choreographic changes. In 1958 Balanchine made the adagio of the *grand pas de deux* a *pas de cinq* by having the ballerina supported by the principal male soloists of the preceding Coffee, Tea, and Candy Cane *divertissements*. Critics deplored this innovation, and the adagio became a *pas de deux* once more. An alteration which has become permanent, however, occurred in 1964 when, instead of treating the Coffee (Arabian) variation as a male solo, Balanchine rechoreographed it as a solo for a lady belly dancer with a diamond

The company of the New York City Ballet. The scenery for this production is by Rouben Ter-Arutunian.

in her navel. Season after season, Balanchine has experimented with tricks of stagecraft. One that never fails to amaze Lincoln Center audiences is employed in the adagio of the *grand pas de deux*. The ballerina, with only fingertip support from her partner, holds an arabesque. Although she is totally motionless, she nevertheless gives the impression that she is moving while standing still, owing to the fact that she has placed her foot upon an otherwise unobtrusive movable disc on the floor which is set into motion when the time comes for the stage illusion.

The New York City *Nutcracker* makes use of the entire company. During the course of the annual long *Nutcracker* seasons at Christmas time, all of the company's principal dancers star on at least one occasion in *The Nutcracker*, and opportunities are also given to some of the talented younger soloists to appear as Sugarplum Fairy, Prince, or Dewdrop. Two separate casts of children—each cast made up of about 40 youngsters—alternate in the roles of children, toys, angels, and mice. Since 1970 David Richardson, a dancer with the company, has been in charge of training and rehearsing the children. By 1975 there were 19 adult dancers in the 90-member company who had started their dancing careers in one or another of the children's roles. Other alumni of *The Nutcracker* children's casts have gone on to fame outside the New York City Ballet. One such is Eliot Feld, today considered one of America's most talented young choreographers, who directs his own Eliot Feld Ballet.

In 1977 the publicity office of the New York City Ballet estimated that the Balanchine *Nutcracker* is seen by more than 100,000 people a year. Of these the majority are children, since *The Nutcracker* has become a holiday treat to which adults like to take their sons and daughters and nephews and nieces. (New York City Ballet staff members suspect that for the elders *The Nutcracker* is also a treat, except that the proprieties of adult behavior make them reluctant to admit it.) Today at the New York State Theater, as in the old days at City Center, auditorium and foyers swarm with children when *The Nutcracker* time comes along. With an enthusiastic and happy audience of unpredictable children, dancers and musicians never know what to expect, and tales are still told of the afternoon when the musicians in the pit were pelted with chocolate kisses by a little boy with a slingshot up in the balcony. More often, however, the children are on their best behavior, and once the ballet gets underway they watch the action with silent wonder.

As Edwin Denby proclaimed after the premiere in 1954, 'New York City Ballet's *Nutcracker* is a smash hit. . . . It is Balanchine's *Oklahoma!*—a family spectacle, large and leisurely, that lasts two hours and sends people home refreshed and happy.' A few people have adopted a sourpuss attitude toward it, including John Martin, the esteemed dance critic of *The New York Times*. Some of his complaints were the standard ones that have been raised against *The Nutcracker* ever since its premiere. 'It is not much of a ballet,' said Martin, 'and all the genius in the world can never make it one. There is no dancing to speak of until the last scene, there is no story line, and no characters to develop.'

Those objections Martin would have raised against any company's *Nutcracker*. What made this production particularly distasteful to him was that he feared it might herald a lowering of artistic standards by the New York City Ballet, which had established a reputation for being at the forefront of the balletic avant-garde. (The company's last new production before the premiere of *The Nutcracker* had been *Opus 34*, an expressionist ballet to atonal music by Arnold Schoenberg.) Martin had no patience with the theory that by offering commercially successful attractions, such as *The Nutcracker*, the New York City Ballet would gain a new audience which in time might develop enough curiosity to see the experimental offerings: 'It is an outworn superstition that by giving people what is inferior you will ultimately win them to what is superior. The sad and terrible result is usually that they become so much more deeply attached to the inferior that it becomes financially impossible to give them anything else.'

Fortunately no aesthetic erosion occurred

Left
Roger Shim in John Neumeier's production for the Royal Winnipeg Ballet in which the setting has been adapted for a birthday party.
Right
Kathleen Duffy in the same production.

at the New York City Ballet. If *The Nut-cracker* dominates programming at Christmas time, at other times during the New York season the company presents its regular repertoire, including its abstractions to such composers as Stravinsky, Hindemith, Ives, and Webern. Other critics would by no means agree with John Martin that Balanchine's *Nutcracker* is choreographically trivial. Indeed its fervent admirers have been constantly astonished at the care that Balanchine has devoted to his staging. For Clive Barnes, 'Balanchine's *Nutcracker* is in a sense a far more *serious* ballet than any other *Nutcracker* we have known.' To support his contention, Barnes cites how Balanchine 'takes the staging of the first scene . . . and lavishes upon it an extraordinary wealth of detail. The acting is naturalistic, and Balanchine has gone to enormous pains to present precisely the leisurely bourgeois existence of the Stahlbaum home.' Arlene Croce, ordinarily a demanding critic, agrees wholeheartedly with Barnes, saying, '*The Nutcracker*, both in conception and in execution, seems to me as nearly flawless a work as the company has ever staged.'

During the past quarter century *Nutcracker*s have proliferated across the North American continent. Today, says Clive Barnes, 'America has *Nutcracker*s like a squirrel has nuts.' Resident professional companies in the great cities of the United States and Canada produce annual *Nutcracker*s, as do the semi-professional and non-professional community companies which are often said to constitute America's grassroots regional ballet movement. Among early *Nutcracker* productions by companies big or small, professional or amateur, are those of Ballet Imperial of Ottawa (1946), the Southern Ballet of Atlanta (1946), Los Angeles Festival Ballet (1951), Capitol Ballet of Washington (1952), Ballet West of Salt Lake City (1955, when the company was known as Utah Civic Ballet), Detroit Severo Ballet (1955), National Ballet of Canada (1956), Macon (Georgia) Ballet Guild (1957), Birmingham Ballet (1957), and the Atlanta Ballet (1958).

The Chinese Dance representing Tea as performed by the Atlanta Ballet.

The non-professional Ballet Imperial of Ottawa helped pioneer *The Nutcracker* in Canada, and today all three major Canadian professional ballet companies have produced it: the National Ballet of Canada in a version by Celia Franca; Les Grands Ballets Canadiens of Montreal in a version by Fernand Nault; and the Royal Winnipeg Ballet in a highly controversial version by John Neumeier. The first full-length South American production was that of Yurek Shabelevski for the Sodre Ballet in Montevideo in 1958, starring Sunny Lorinczi and Raul Severo. That same year Vassili Lambrinos choreographed a *Nutcracker* 'in the round' for the Buenos Aires Arena Theater.

Usually *The Nutcracker* is produced because company directors wish to stage it or feel that their audiences wish to see it. Another commonly advanced reason for staging *The Nutcracker* is that it has been requested as a special Christmas treat by the conductor of the local symphony orchestra. Many companies outside New York, unable to afford an orchestra throughout the entire year, perform most of the time to recorded music— but not when they do *The Nutcracker*, for *The Nutcracker* seems to be performed to live musical accompaniment more often than any other single work in the American ballet repertoire. The accompanying groups of

musicians can range from the members of an amateur orchestral society to some of the leading symphony orchestras of the United States. For example, the lavish production of *The Nutcracker* staged by the Minnesota Dance Theater of Minneapolis is annually accompanied by the Minnesota Orchestra.

Most *Nutcracker*s outside New York are designed for a specific local theater and are never taken on tour, simply because they are so elaborate. Some *Nutcracker*s do travel. Every Christmas the Eglevsky Ballet of Long Island takes its staging to several cities in upstate New York, even though that production requires not only a full *corps de ballet* of adults, but a special children's ensemble, complete with tutors to make sure the youngsters do their homework while they are absent from their regular schools.

Although *The Nutcracker* is invariably a

Left
The Sugarplum Fairy and her cavalier in the *pas de deux* in the production by the Cincinnati Ballet Company.
Above
The mechanical dolls in the American Ballet Theater production.
Right
Mère Gigogne is called Mother Ginger in the Cincinnati Ballet Company production.

crowd pleaser and often a money maker as well, there are ballet directors who fear that its very popularity makes it a millstone that can impede a company's growth. Often a company will spend much of the autumn rehearsing *The Nutcracker*, while the weeks immediately following the New Year will be devoted to recovering from the strain of having to dance one, and only one, ballet night after night. In such cases too much of a theatrical season will have been taken up by *The Nutcracker*, its preparation and its aftereffects. Some directors also fear that audiences may come to demand that every ballet in the repertoire be as innocuous and as scenically opulent as *The Nutcracker*—something which is both financially impractical and artistically undesirable. Conceivably audiences conditioned to *The Nutcracker* might lose interest in intellectually demanding ballets that company directors might consider, aesthetically speaking, the treasures of the repertoire. Despite arguments and objections (and some of the very choreographers and directors who stage *The Nutcracker* argue in private most persuasively against its omnipresence), it looks as though *The Nutcracker* will remain a part of American holiday celebrations.

Many current American *Nutcracker*s are related in one way or another to earlier productions. Former members of the New York City Ballet and the Ballet Russe de Monte Carlo have set the work for other companies in ways that recall the stagings in which they used to appear. The Cincinnati Ballet's production, for instance, is by Frederic Franklin, Moscelyne Larkin, and Roman Jasinski, all former members of the Ballet Russe. Balletgoers with long memories say that much of it resembles both the 'after Ivanov' version by Fedorova for the Ballet Russe and the apparently similar 'after Ivanov' version by Sergueeff for the Vic-Wells, although in some of its details it suggests the Balanchine version, which has had an all-pervasive influence in the United States. Few producers of *The Nutcracker* are content to make their staging a mere carbon copy of one in the past. Therefore the Cincinnati Ballet has hit upon the idea of setting its *Nutcracker* in nine-

Michael Hackett as Madame Bonbonnière, Michele Abraham as the little girl Marie and Andrew Rist as the Nutcracker with the company of the Minnesota Dance Theater in the Kingdom of Jam and Marzipan Sweets in Act II.

teenth-century Cincinnati, a conceit which wreaks no real havoc upon the ballet since the original *Nutcracker* was set in Germany and Cincinnati was settled by German immigrants who profoundly influenced local architecture, interior decoration, and cuisine. That this *Nutcracker* could be termed a uniquely Cincinnati *Nutcracker* made it possible when it was first staged in 1974 for the Cincinnati Ballet to receive substantial financial grants from Cincinnati business firms and philanthropical foundations, including Frisch's Restaurants and the Corbett Foundation and the Charles B Levinson Foundation.

The Atlanta Ballet is currently directed by Robert Barnett, the original soloist in the Trepak *divertissement* at the premiere of the New York City Ballet's *Nutcracker* in 1954. It is not surprising, then, that its *Nutcracker* is indebted to that of Balanchine. The Pennsylvania Ballet production is another of those which, at least in its *divertissements*, shows the influence of Balanchine, but it, too, has its special touches. A Snow Queen and a Snow King have been added to the winter forest scene, dancing choreography by Robert Rodham. And the entire first act has been restaged by Osvaldo Riofrancos, a play and opera director. Riofrancos makes much of the scary events in Clara's nightmare. Indeed he dwells upon them so much that *New Yorker* critic Arlene Croce, when she journeyed to Philadelphia to see the production, called the first act 'appalling in its grotesquerie' and cited as an example, 'at one point several large white plastic rats crept about on a table in a blue light.' Also in this version, Drosselmeyer exists only in Clara's imagination and is seen only by her; symbolically, he represents a sort of wise man searching for a child of truth and beauty.

The role of Drosselmeyer has been expanded in a number of productions. In the version by Paul Curtis and Shawn Stuart for the San Jose Dance Theater—an all-volunteer, amateur community organization—Drosselmeyer becomes the key figure in the ballet, riding a grandfather clock to start Clara's dream, leading her into the Candy Kingdom, and taking her back to the parlor

Nathalia Makarova as Clara in the American Ballet Theater production.
Upper inset
Drosselmeyer with a mechanical doll and the company of the Minnesota Dance Theater in the production choreographed by Loyce Houlton.
Lower inset
The company of the Minnesota Dance Theater in Act I.

when it is time to wake up in the morning.

Similarly Drosselmeyer is emphasized in a production that Loyce Houlton has choreographed for the Minnesota Dance Theater, a professional company. Here he seems to symbolize all the awe and wonderment inherent in a child's attitude toward the magical and the unknown, and Houlton has conceived him as a dancing conjurer. Houlton also makes the Mouse King a plum part by reintroducing him in the second act, where he makes a last effort to snatch back his crown. Some of the fantastic events in Clara's dream are prefigured in the events of the party scene when she is still awake; thus Drosselmeyer, who has a shrewd understanding of his godchildren's temperaments, gives Clara's naughty brother a toy rat—scarcely a typical Christmas gift, but one peculiarly suited to this bratty little boy. Houlton's production, a lavish one that is staged annually, is entirely her own choreography, except for the *grand pas de deux*, which in some years is danced in the traditional Ivanov version and in other years in a version by Houlton.

Other choreographers have modified the roles of various characters. In a version that Richard Englund once produced for the Birmingham Ballet of Alabama the problem of expanding the roles of ballerina and *premier danseur* was solved by making the Sugarplum Fairy and her cavalier Clara's dream visions of her own mother and father. Englund saw no reason why Clara could not have young parents or why, being a happy child of a happy home, she could not envision her parents as rulers of a magic kingdom. This conception gave the leading dancers one act of dramatic mime (as the parents) and one act of classical virtuosity (as the Sugarplum Fairy and Cavalier).

Scene from Act I of the
1967 production by the
Minnesota Dance
Theater.

Breaking with Convention

Critic Marcia B Siegel once observed, 'To some people *The Nutcracker* is a disease or a curse. To some it's just another holiday chore. To thousands of screaming kids it's the event of the year. I guess the only people without preconceived notions about *The Nutcracker* are four years old.' With its contrasts between dreaming and waking, its emphasis upon food, and its mice and its magic, *The Nutcracker* invites commentators to spin theoretical webs in an attempt to answer such questions as, 'What does it all mean?' or 'Just why is it that *The Nutcracker* is so popular?'

From the standpoint of practical stagecraft, there are a number of reasons why choreographers enjoy staging *The Nutcracker* and audiences enjoy watching it. For one thing, despite recurrent complaints about the banality of the scenario, the ballet does possess considerable internal variety. With their abundance of realistic gesture, the pantomime scenes of the first act might be termed earthbound: certainly most of the movement in them is what ballet teachers call *terre à terre* movement, movement in which the feet hardly leave the ground. However, the fantastic dances of the dream

Vergie Derman and Julian Hosking in the Arabian Dance from the Royal Ballet production.

omitting the battle with the mice. What made the production unusual was that Karpova was really a man (dancer and choreographer Antony Bassae) and all other women's roles were also performed by men.

Les Ballets Trockadero de Monte Carlo is a travesty ballet company in which men dance ballerina roles. Yet this organization's productions are something more than female impersonation routines, for the Trockadero is out to poke affectionate fun at the conventions of classical ballet. At its best, the Trockadero is so wickedly accurate in its parody that Arlene Croce, a critic ordinarily not given to levity, wrote a lengthy essay analyzing the company's brand of fooling. Croce found that matters of weight and gravity helped explain why the Tockadero's antics were funny. 'A heavy thing trying to become light is automatically funnier than a light thing trying to become heavy,' she said. Since balletic custom requires women to appear lighter on stage than men, the sight of muscular men doing things ordinarily associated with sylph-like women is preposterous to behold. Croce found that Bassae impersonating the ballerina Karpova was 'built like a pug version of Lou Costello, and on point looks a little like a bulldog standing on its hind legs.'

Right
Scene from Act II of the New York City Ballet production which was designed by Horace Armistead in 1954.
Below
One of Mother Ginger's children emerges from her large hoop skirt (New York City Ballet).

Perhaps the best way to indicate the tone
of a Trockadero performance is to quote its
own program notes for *The Nutcracker*:

Act I

Scene 1

After much heartburning and soul-searching, Mama and Papa put the final touches to the family tree. The children are summoned to admire their handiwork; Clara's amazement and delight know no bounds at this radical departure from the traditional pink aluminium.

Clara's darling little playmates join her in gleeful raptures, while Fritz and his dubiously acquired pals from the Junior Health Club remain unimpressed. Soon the guests, stepping delicately over the children, arrive for the Annual Christmas Encounter Group but permit themselves to be persuaded to a tiny tipple for the Holidays.

As the guests are mingling and making themselves at home the peculiar Herr Drosselmeyer enters with his ridiculous nephew. He brings in a doll to amuse the children; this, however, is not an unqualified success. Shattered by disappointment, Clara lapses into her first pre-adolescent vaporish spasm. She is inexplicably consoled by a hideously ugly and utterly useless nutcracker, with which she is presented by Herr Drosselmeyer.

A ceremonious but gay *marche* follows. As the adult guests repair to the bar a fight breaks out among the children, wherein Clara suffers her second pre-adolescent trauma of the evening when the nutcracker breaks. The guests take this as a subtle hint and depart *en masse*, while some lively diversion is still to be found along Piterskaya Street.

Mama bundles the disconsolate Clara off to bed.

Scene 2

Clara steals back downstairs to take a last longing peek at her wounded nutcracker. Lurking in the darkness is the sinister but lovable old Herr Drosselmeyer, who invites Clara to go with him to a few mysterious places. Startled but intrigued, Clara accepts.

They are magically borne to the Kingdom of the Snows, where they are first welcomed, then engulfed, and then sped on their way by the beautiful Snow Queen and her beautiful Attendant Flakes.

Act II

Leaving the Snow Kingdom, Clara and Herr Drosselmeyer arrive at Konfiturenburg, the Kingdom of the Sweets. They are greeted by Mother Ginger, who shocks the delicately nurtured Clara by lifting her skirts to produce a wriggling horde of ethnic *divertissements*: these proceed to leap about and cavort for Clara's amusement. The highlight of the entertainment is provided by the Sugarplum Fairy, who condescends to dance the *grand pas de deux* with a cavalier bearing a suspicious resemblance to that nephew of Herr Drosselmeyer.

All the Sweets then gather for the climactic *Grande Valse*. Mindful of her mother's injunction against accepting candy from odd little old men, Clara bids a reluctant farewell to the Candy People.

If the Trockadero's *Nutcracker* is a comic approach to the ballet, other productions have been both unusual and serious. When Nicholas Beriozoff choreographed Festival Ballet's first *Nutcracker* in 1950, he was content to follow traditional lines. Not quite so traditional was the version he staged in 1969 for the Zurich Ballet (starring Gaye Fulton and Ben de Rochemont). In this staging Drosselmeyer is not the usual old crank or codger, but an attractive young magician. Beriozoff also made *The Nutcracker* even grander than usual by adding to it other music borrowed from Tchaikovsky's orchestral suites and from *The Sleeping Beauty*.

The London Festival Ballet acquired a new *Nutcracker* by Ronald Hynd (1931–   )

in 1976 which was as unconventional as that company's previous versions had been conventional. Designed by Peter Docherty, it was premiered in Liverpool on 9 November 1976, with Eva Evdokimova and Peter Breuer as Louise and Karl, the first London performance occurring 27 December 1976. Possibly to satisfy those complainers who wail that the plot of *The Nutcracker* is so simple as to seem almost infantile, Hynd complicated the story line considerably. In some—but by no means all, or even most— *Nutcracker* productions, Clara has an older sister named Louise. Hynd took this character, heretofore a somewhat nebulous personage, and made her his production's ballerina, Clara thereby becoming a secondary

Madame Bonbonnière and her brood of children appear from under her skirt in a London Festival Ballet production.

ballerina role. Drosselmeyer's nephew Karl was also Louise's lover (as well as being the prince in the *divertissements*), and the Christmas Eve dream was apparently dreamed by both Clara and Louise (quite a feat, some London critics noted). Into the Christmas party, usually all sweetness and light, Hynd introduced an ill-tempered snobbish family among the guests, the von Rattensteins. Despite their unpleasantness, Frau Stahlbaum is impressed by their wealth and wishes Louise to marry Herman von Rattenstein who (as one might predict, given Hynd's schematization) becomes King Rat in the nightmare. As if these complications were not enough, Hynd also added a comic female servant to the Stahlbaum household.

Another feature of the Hynd production is that objects and incidents in the first act reappear in a fantastic form during the dream. Thus a bouquet of flowers left on the floor after the party gives rise to the Waltz of the Flowers, and because brother Fritz entertains guests by dancing a hornpipe, he reappears in the dream as the commander of the ship that crosses the Lemonade Sea to the Candy Kingdom.

Odd though these tinkerings are, the versions of Beriozoff and Hynd pale in their idiosyncrasies when they are compared with the *Nutcracker*s of Roland Petit (1924–), Rudolf Nureyev (1938–), Mikhail Baryshnikov (1948–), John Cranko (1927–1973), and John Neumeier (1942–). Each of these choreographers takes his own special view of *The Nutcracker*, a view which is, if nothing else, original, even controversial.

Like the Hynd *Nutcracker*, Roland Petit's *Nutcracker* for Les Ballets de Marseille dates from 1976. Designed by Ezio Frigerio, this version is set in the 1880s and stresses the awakening to love of the adolescent Clara. Drosselmeyer (who plays a greater role than usual) leads her to a love which is at first a fancy and then a reality by giving her first the toy nutcracker and then introducing her to his nephew, the lover of her dreams. Petit's Drosselmeyer is no old gentleman, but a very debonair fellow who entertains party guests with conjuring tricks and with his ability to do a tap dance. Petit turns the snowflakes of the winter scene into skaters and is able to bring the members of the vocal chorus on stage by dressing them up as Salvation Army lassies. France being the land of *l'amour*, Petit has introduced into the *divertissements* a few touches that might strike dancegoers from other lands as being typically French: thus, in the Mirlitons' *divertissement* a shepherdess is pursued everywhere by an amorous shepherd boy, and the Arabian Dance becomes a solo for a handsome young man wearing only a loincloth. Petit's innovations extend to the music, for he has incorporated into this *Nutcracker* part of a trio by E T A Hoffmann, which is used as a solo for Drosselmeyer. The cast included Elisabetta Terabust as Clara, Rudy Bryans as Drossel-meyer, and Denys Ganio as the Nutcracker Prince.

The Gallic touches make the Petit *Nutcracker* a ballet for sophisticated adults as well as for children. Rudolf Nureyev also tried to make his *Nutcracker* an adult entertainment. He first produced it for the Royal Swedish Ballet in Stockholm on 17 November 1967. This staging was, in effect, something of a tryout for the version which, designed by Nicholas Georgiadis, entered the Royal Ballet's repertoire at Covent Garden on 29 February 1968, with Leslie Edwards as Dr. Stahlbaum, Betty Kavanagh as Frau Stahlbaum, Merle Park as Clara, Keith Martin as Fritz, Ann Jenner as Louisa,

Right
Clara and the Nutcracker Prince leave the Land of Ice and Snow on their way to the Kingdom of Sweets in a London Festival Ballet production.
Below
Christine Hammond as Clara in the Prologue in a London Festival Ballet production.

and Nureyev himself in his strikingly conceived reinterpretation of Drosselmeyer. Except for the male variation in the second act, which was borrowed from Vainonen's Leningrad version, the choreography was entirely by Nureyev. However, Nureyev also borrowed the Russian notion of having Clara played by an adult dancer so that she, rather than some ballerina who suddenly appears out of nowhere, may dance the climactic second act *pas de deux*. Nureyev's arrangement of this *pas de deux* was unusual in that it contained many unison steps for the ballerina and *danseur* which were exciting to watch when performed by a well-matched pair.

It was not technical ingenuities such as these that made the ballet a much debated attraction, nor was it really any obvious change that Nureyev had made in the basic plot. Essentially Nureyev's *Nutcracker* told the expected story of Christmas party, dream, mouse battle, and journey to Candyland. Nureyev even took pains to present explicitly one event that most producers are content merely to imply: after the *divertissements* a scene transformation brings Clara back to the house where she is shown waking up. But it was the decidedly peculiar interpretation that Nureyev made of the familiar events that made his *Nutcracker* so unusual.

The one single feature of his production

Freya Dominic and Jonathan Kelly in the foreground with Kathryn Wade and Christian Addams dance the flower scene from a London Festival Ballet production.

that might be said to epitomize Nureyev's whole approach to *The Nutcracker* is that he turns the grotesque Drosselmeyer of the first act into the handsome Prince of the second. Nureyev presumably reasons that this old man who is simultaneously mystifying, awesome, and fascinating to Clara at the party has so dominated her waking thoughts that he will also dominate her dreams. And since it is Clara and Drosselmeyer (rejuvenated as the Prince), and not the Sugarplum Fairy and Cavalier, who dance the *pas de deux*, the *pas de deux* becomes a symbol of the extent to which Clara is attracted to Drosselmeyer.

Mary Clarke coolly dismissed all this as rubbish: 'My biggest quarrel with Nureyev's version is that almost nothing is plausible and almost every dramatic point is missed.' Other critics started invoking the name of Sigmund Freud. Said Marcia B Marks of *Dance Magazine*, 'Rightly, Nureyev's *Nutcracker* might be reviewed by a psychoanalyst as well as a dance critic. How does one explain its recurrent brutality?' Images of cruelty do abound in this *Nutcracker*. At the very start of the first act, on their way to the Stahlbaums' Christmas party little boys roughhouse on the street with a woman carrying a Christmas tree, and another boy hits some little girls as they pass. Some of the adults at the party are choreographically caricatured and the Grandfather Dance is performed by grotesque, almost senile, dodderers. During Nureyev's unusually violent war of the toys and the mice, rats devour two little girls and, in their attack upon Clara, rip off her skirt. But the defeat of the rats does not bring calm, for in their journey to the Kingdom of Sweets Clara and Drosselmeyer pass through a grotto inhabited by malicious bats that turn out to be Clara's own relatives who have acquired nightmarish shapes.

With the *divertissements*, calm arrives at last. Nureyev gives the suite of dances unity by having them performed in Clara's own toy theater by her favorite dolls. Several of the dances attracted particularly favorable comment: the Mirliton Dance conceived as an eighteenth-century pastoral, the Chinese Dance for a male trio of Oriental tumblers, and the Arabian Dance, during which a sultan lording it over his harem and eating sweetmeats fed to him by his wives has a bag of gold stolen from his pocket by some belly dancers. For all their wit and charm, however, the *divertissements* do little to affect the somber mood of Nureyev's production as a whole.

There are those who defend Nureyev's conception by arguing that many fairy tales contain scenes of brutality, that children's behavior is rarely angelic, and that children may harbor ambivalent feelings toward their adult relatives. It can also be asked whether *The Nutcracker* is the proper theatrical vehicle for the expression of these ideas. Don McDonagh, for one, thinks it ludicrous to bring 'the agony of the analyst's couch' into *The Nutcracker*. According to McDonagh the relationship between Clara and Drosselmeyer is totally unconvincing: 'Clara is as impressionable as any girl her age but would not be sexually obsessed with a limping old man with an eye patch who looks like Long John Silver dragging his way around her living room.' Most importantly, the tone of

Nureyev's choreography in no way harmonizes with that of Tchaikovsky's score: 'If the Tchaikovsky music is used, there is no escaping its mellifluous tonality, and the attempt to make it bear the psychological weight of tortured sexuality that Nureyev has unloaded upon its unwary shoulders is a dreadful mistake.'

Since 1968 Nureyev has choreographed other *Nutcrackers* for La Scala, Milan, and the Teatro Colón in Buenos Aires, and has fussed with details of his Royal Ballet production. He has added a new romantic *pas*

The Nutcracker and his army of toy soldiers battle with the mice in an American Ballet Theater production.
Inset
The Nutcracker and the Mouse King in a duel in the same production.

de deux for Clara and her Drosselmeyer–
Prince at the beginning of the second act,
replacing a boat journey across a Lemonade
Sea that was considered an indifferent piece
of stagecraft. He has also attempted to
strengthen the psychological links between
the first and second acts by having some of
the dancers who portray Clara's relatives reappear in the *divertissements*. Clara's sister and
brother turn up in the Spanish Dance, her
mother and father are cast in the Trepak, and
her grandfather is the tyrannical, but gullible,
old sultan in the Arabian Dance.

One trouble with any ballet production
famous for its oddities is that the production
may become such a familiar part of the repertoire that its oddities will seem common-
place. There are those London critics who
feel that Nureyev's *Nutcracker* has not worn
well over the years. Seeing the production
in 1976, James Monahan sadly noted that
'The sub-Freudian touches . . . looked sillier
with time and Nureyev's choreography
seems increasingly maladroit.'

As in the Nureyev version, Drosselmeyer
dominates the *Nutcracker* choreographed by
Mikhail Baryshnikov for American Ballet
Theater, with scenery by Boris Aronson,
costumes by Frank Thompson, and lighting
by Jennifer Tipton. This *Nutcracker* was
premiered in Washington, DC, on 21 December 1976 with Marianna Tcherkassky as
Clara, Alexander Minz as Drosselmeyer, and

Baryshnikov as the Nutcracker Prince.
Baryshnikov, the young dancer from the
Leningrad Kirov Ballet who chose to remain
in the West rather than to return to Russia,
had astounded audiences in America and
Europe with his breathtaking virtuosity as a
performer, but before receiving the commission to stage *The Nutcracker* had never
undertaken a piece of choreography. Like
his fellow emigré from Leningrad, Rudolf
Nureyev, he borrowed a bit from the Vainonen version—in this case, the choreography
for the Snowflake Waltz. Otherwise, the
ballet was entirely his own. There were those
who felt that Baryshnikov, being an untried
choreographer, should not have been assigned a two-act work as his first project.
Even so, a number of critics, including
Dance Magazine's David Vaughan, considered at least much of the first act to be 'un-
failingly musical' with 'many felicitous
touches.' Vaughan, however, was forced to
add that, in his opinion, 'the second act is
inferior in every way.'

An explanation of why this is so may be
found by examining how Baryshnikov
works out his conception of *The Nutcracker*
from scene to scene. Like the Nureyev version, the Baryshnikov *Nutcracker* is concerned with the psychology of children,
especially with the way adults sometimes
strike impressionable children as being
simultaneously frightening and attractive.

Yet Baryshnikov disdains the psychological excesses of Nureyev. In his version (in which all children's roles are played by adults and Clara is the star ballerina role), Baryshnikov emphasizes the gap between childhood and adulthood by having Clara's nutcracker broken at the party not by her brother, but by a tipsy adult guest, making the incident one of those casual and thoughtless small acts of cruelty that adults may perform and in so doing deeply wound a child. No wonder, then, that in Clara's nightmare the adults return transformed into the marauding mice. But if adults can seem cruel, they can also seem wondrous to children—children long for the day when they, too, are grown up—and Baryshnikov's *Nutcracker* is a ballet about some of the joys and the pangs of growing up.

Overseeing this process for Clara is her godfather, Drosselmeyer, also a magician. Early in the first act he makes tiny dolls grow bigger and come alive, and Clara wishes her nutcracker would also undergo a similar metamorphosis. In her dream Drosselmeyer comes to her and seems to say, 'You wanted your nutcracker to grow up, did you? Look, I am going to give you what you begged for as a reward for your kindness and love for the nutcracker.' And he changes the nutcracker into a handsome prince. Drosselmeyer makes one further appearance in the ballet, an appearance which has caused more critical debate than any other incident in the Baryshnikov production. Because it occurs in the second act, this incident is one of the reasons why some commentators consider the second act distinctly inferior to the first. Drosselmeyer participates in what would normally be called the *grand pas de deux*, but which is here, because of his presence in it, something of a *pas de trois*. He steps between Clara and her Prince in an attempt to lead Clara away from the land of dreams and back to reality. Dramatically this can be easily justified, since the sequence can serve as a reminder that for Clara, on the verge of adolescence, the dream of childhood is nearly over. Choreographically the innovation may be less defensible because the intrusion of a third person prevents the *pas de*

Cranko choreographed a *Nutcracker* that told a whole new story of his own invention. This version takes place not at Christmas, but on Clara's birthday and Clara is a teen-aged girl fully old enough to fall in love with a handsome soldier. This innovation helps make casting especially easy. Even in those traditional productions in which Clara is played by an adult ballerina, if Clara is still supposed to be a child, she can be portrayed only by dancers who are short of stature. If Clara is a teen-ager, the role can be danced by a ballerina of almost any height. Another peculiarity is that Cranko has invented what amounts to a female Drosselmeyer. Instead of a mysterious godfather, there is an eccentric old aunt who is not only Clara's godmother, but her fairy godmother. It is she who manipulates the events in the plot.

deux from attaining a spacious and exultant climax befitting the music that Tchaikovsky has written for it: the music soars, but the dance action is cramped. If one is willing to accept this intrusion of Drosselmeyer one may notice, as critic Tobi Tobias has noticed, that the scene is very carefully thought out. Tobias cites several instances where subtle dramatic touches amidst the otherwise academically classical choreography remind one that Clara is still a child: for example, when she leaps toward her Prince, one expects a spectacular lift. Instead he cradles her protectively in his arms as though she were a little girl.

However fantastic, or even (to some tastes) perverse, the variations may be that Nureyev and Baryshnikov play upon the theme of *The Nutcracker*, the resultant productions are still recognizable as *The Nutcracker*. It is even possible to argue that, for all its unconventional details, the Baryshnikov *Nutcracker* is basically traditional in spirit. With its overt attempts at psychologizing, the Nureyev *Nutcracker* is undeniably odd, yet even it does not totally abandon the familiar scenario. However, there have been a few *Nutcracker*s which have not only jettisoned the expected story, but which have nothing at all to do with Christmas. And neither do they have much to do with nutcrackers.

For the Stuttgart Ballet in 1966 John

When the handsome soldier starts flirting
with all the girls except Clara, who really
loves him, the godmother contrives to make
the others look preposterous and, to dazzle
the soldier's eyes still further, takes him and
Clara on a magic journey, after which he discovers that he does indeed love Clara.

This version was considered sufficiently
interesting to be widely discussed by German balletgoers, but critics, by and large, did
not rate it as one of Cranko's major creations,
and although the Stuttgart Ballet has been
successful on its several tours of America,
its complete *Nutcracker* has never figured in
the touring repertoire. The company's first
New York season in 1969, however, did include the *Nutcracker divertissements*. They
were not a success, Arlene Croce going so
far as to call them 'pop ballet on its lowest

level of vulgarization.' One of the *divertissements*, a buffoons' dance for blackamoors
(played by white dancers in blackface),
proved something of a sociological embarrassment in New York, and they were later
transformed into whitefaced clowns.

One of the members of the cast of Cranko's
1966 *Nutcracker* was John Neumeier, the
young American dancer and choreographer
who became director of the Frankfurt Ballet
in 1969. In Frankfurt the ballet had to share
an orchestra and a production budget with
the local opera company. Therefore Neumeier was always looking for ways in which
he could stage new works that would utilize
pieces of scenery from the company ware-
house and scores with which the musicians
were already familiar. Neumeier's predeces-
sor as ballet director in Frankfurt, Todd
Bolender, had once staged a *Nutcracker*. The
scenery by Werner Schachteli still existed
and the orchestra still remembered the music.
Why not produce *The Nutcracker*? thought
Neumeier.

But as he began rehearsals he found himself discarding one traditional idea after
another. At last, perhaps heartened by
Cranko's precedent, he discarded the story
altogether and started afresh. As Baryshnikov was to do several years later, Neumeier
made *The Nutcracker* a ballet about growing
up, and his heroine (called Maria and played
by an adult) was conceived as a twelve-year-

Above
The Nutcracker battling
with the Mouse King in
the American Ballet
Theater production.
Above left
In the same production
the adults from the
party scene are trans-
formed into mice who
attack the soldiers.
Left
Marianna Tcherkassky
as Clara in an American
Ballet Theater
production.

old girl, a girl who was no longer a child but not quite an adolescent. Neumeier also gave new prominence to Maria's usually nebulous sister, Louise. Like Cranko, Neumeier changed the setting of the ballet from a Christmas party to a birthday party, justifying the change by saying, 'Birthdays for children are times of dreaming about the things one wants and the things one wants to do, and on her birthday twelve-year-old Maria does just that.'

Maria's older sister Louise (a ballet dancer) brings Drosselmeyer as a guest to Maria's birthday party. Drosselmeyer turns out to be the ballet master of the local theater. Maria's brother, who attends a military academy, brings his captain and some of the other cadets. They present Maria with a military doll bearing a resemblance to the captain (the only object in this version that could even remotely be called a nutcracker), and before the party is over Maria has fallen in love with the captain, who happens to be attracted to Louise. Drosselmeyer's birthday gift for Maria is a pair of point shoes and he even consents to give her a brief dancing lesson. When the party is over, Maria puts on the point shoes and tries to remember the steps Drosselmeyer taught her. Her attempts at dancing fail and she falls sadly asleep.

She then dreams that Drosselmeyer comes to take her to a ballet rehearsal at the theater. What is more, the handsome captain at the real-life military school has been transformed into Louise's partner, the *premier danseur* of the ballet company. Magically Maria discovers that she, too, can dance and she dances with the captain (to the Cinderella *divertissement* that Tchaikovsky wrote for *The Sleeping Beauty*, but which is seldom used in contemporary stagings of that ballet). She also learns—and this is a sign that she is growing up—that dancing is hard work and that Drosselmeyer is a stern taskmaster.

Neumeier's *Nutcracker* was premiered by the Frankfurt Ballet on 21 October 1971 with Marianne Kruuse as Maria, Persephone Samarapoulo as Louise, Egon Madsen as

Nicholas Johnson as Fritz in Act I of Ronald Hynd's production for the London Festival Ballet in 1976 dances to a hornpipe.

Artists of London Festival Ballet in the party scene in Act I of the Hynd production.

Günther (the Captain), Maximo Barra as Fritz, and the highly regarded character dancer Max Midinet as Drosselmeyer. German critic Horst Koegler considered the production a considerable achievement. If the strictly classical dances were somewhat weak, they were compensated for by the excellence of the dramatic and character dances. Koegler (and other critics on both sides of the Atlantic) considered the conception of Drosselmeyer remarkable. This eccentric ballet teacher could easily have stepped from the pages of a Hoffmann story. Even if this man was something of a madman, it was also clear that he was totally devoted to the art of classical ballet and so he deserved one's respect, even as one smiled at his outlandishness. That was precisely what Neumeier had intended. He says of the character, 'My Drosselmeyer is an incarnation of Petipa, or of Balanchine, or of any great ballet master, mad about the ballet, passionate about dancing.'

Unlike the Cranko *Nutcracker*, Neumeier's idiosyncratic reinterpretation became enormously popular and much in demand by other companies for their repertoires. In 1972 he mounted his *Nutcracker* with much praised new scenery by Jürgen Rose for the Royal Winnipeg Ballet, which has toured the production with great success; in 1973 Neumeier choreographed *The Nutcracker* again for Munich's Ballet of the Bavarian State Opera. There are balletgoers who cluck disapprovingly over Neumeier's changes, but other balletgoers enjoy them very much. Since this version has so little to do with a nutcracker, even its admirers sometimes feel constrained to ask, as Horst Koegler once did ask, 'Why call it any longer *The Nutcracker* . . . ?'

Ballet directors the world over have an answer to that question. 'You call it *The Nutcracker*,' they might say, 'because the mere title, *The Nutcracker*, always attracts audiences.'

The problem does remain, however, of how wise it is to make changes in *The Nutcracker* and, if changes are to be made, how extensive those changes ought to be. Is the

Above
The battle with the mice in an American Ballet Theater production.
Left
Rudolf Nureyev as Drosselmeyer in his own production for the Royal Ballet, first staged at Covent Garden on 29 February 1968.

Petipa scenario truly as naive as scoffers allege? Or is there something lovable about it, dramatic warts and all? Perhaps it might be best to let British critic James Monahan have the last word on the issue. Monahan, a veteran balletgoer who has been sitting through *Nutcracker*s since the 1930s, once put the matter this way: 'On the one hand, I am all for renovating *The Nutcracker*, almost no matter how odd the renovations may be. The original scenario of 1892 is dotty and Ivanov's original choreography, all except the final *grand pas de deux*, is long since lost . . . so why not have a go at it? I see it as a Christmas quiz for choreographers: how would *you* produce *The Nutcracker*? [Prize for the most bizarre answer.] And the assorted answers are, I find, entertaining. On the other hand, I believe that when the innovators have had their way with it and we have approved this exotic caprice and tut-tutted about that one, our favor will return to the oldest version we know, the one which is nearest to what Nicholas Sergueeff brought with him, in Stepanov notation, when he came West from Bolshevik Russia over 50 years ago. Not just because age and nostalgia have made it precious but because, however silly its scenario may be, it is the simplest, the most childlike, the most satisfying. Other versions are the passing fancies; this one is wife and home—a refuge when the romping is over.'

Designing
the Ballet

A ballet about magic, *The Nutcracker* often looks most magical at performances when choreography, music, and dancing are enhanced by the magic of stage design. Superficially the ballet may seem to pose no problem at all for a designer. Three basic settings are called for, and there is no ambiguity whatsoever about what locales they are to represent. First, there is a family parlor; next, there is a snow-covered forest; and finally, there is the palace of the Sugarplum Fairy.

Because the scenic requirements for *The Nutcracker* may appear to be simple, designers may feel that, provided their settings in some way depict the three locales, they can let their imaginations soar in wild flights of fancy. They might make the party scene an example of mundane realism and then amaze audiences with a cubist or surrealist Land of Sweets. They might introduce Freudian symbolism into the décor, or emphasize the scenario's references to food by making everything on stage resemble a larger-than-life edible, they might borrow from many different historical periods, or they might invent a period style—complete to the last detail of hair-dos and interior decoration—entirely their own. The range of fancy effects designers contrive includes magic Christmas trees, magic beds, and blizzards with genuine-looking falling snow.

Left Elizabeth Anderton and David Drew in the Russian Dance for the Royal Ballet.
Below Costume design by Nicholas Georgiadis for the Russian dancer.

While *The Nutcracker* may be a challenge to a designer's imagination, it is not necessarily so in the way that a designer may at first think. *The Nutcracker* is not so simple a ballet that it permits a designer's fancy to run loose on any path he may choose. Any designer of *The Nutcracker* will soon encounter problems comparable to those faced by any choreographer who attempts to stage this ballet. As a matter of fact, as Peter Williams (who writes about both art and ballet) once observed, *The Nutcracker* 'is a damned difficult ballet to design.' And why? Because *The Nutcracker* 'is essentially a ballet that must be designed through a child's eyes because virtually nothing happens. It is an abysmally constructed work, in fact it is hardly a story at all. It is just a little girl's dream completely lacking the brilliant surrealism of that Alice who went to Wonderland.' If Williams is correct in warning a designer against being too sophisticated, perhaps a warning should also be made against being too sweetly sentimental, since *The Nutcracker*, if it is to succeed at all, must seem childlike and not childish.

Many designers have tried their hand at *The Nutcracker*—and with varied results. Perhaps some of the failures should be mentioned first, so that one may understand a few of the ways in which designers are likely to go wrong. The first staging to go wrong may have been the original production of 1892 designed by M Botcharov and K-M Ivanov. At least Alexandre Benois thought it went wrong. He considered the décor for the Stahlbaums' house 'stupid, coarse, heavy and dark.' The original designers apparently also indulged in an 'in' joke that made Benois exclaim in his memoirs, 'How absurd the kind of fresco portraits of Tchaikovsky, Petipa and the rest of them on the walls!'

Most contemporary critics think that Cecil Beaton went wrong in his designs for the 1951 production choreographed by Frederick Ashton for the Sadler's Wells Theatre Ballet. In some respects this ought to have been an easy and rewarding version to design because Ashton dispensed with all traces of narrative, making the ballet an essentially plotless suite of dances instead. Therefore, or so it would seem, a designer could indulge in any number of caprices or extravagances. Beaton, the critics thought, overindulged. Some of his costumes, in the rococo manner, were difficult to dance in, the participants in the Waltz of the Flowers having to wear particularly awkward—and enormous—headdresses. Of the two settings he provided, the one for the wintry forest was in a splotchy black and white style, while that for the Land of Sweets was such a riot of color that the London *Times* was reminded of 'the nightmare one might expect after a surfeit of green Chartreuse, claret and scallops.'

Beaton's production was not the first that came to grief by trying to be too chic. The same charge could be raised against the panels carried about by the dancers in Fyodor Lopukhov's acrobatic Russian production of the 1920s and of the designs that William Chappell (under the pseudonym of Alexeieff) created for Boris Romanov's production for Les Ballets de Monte Carlo in the 1930s. Arnold L Haskell found Chappell's décor 'a nightmare blending of modernism and the sugary.' True, it did fit Romanov's new choreography 'like a glove,' yet both choreography and décor were 'in continual dispute with the music and the theme.'

There are times when *The Nutcracker* designs can be very beautiful and still seem inappropriate to the ballet. Several critics

think that Nicholas Georgiadis' décor for Rudolf Nureyev's Royal Ballet production is blessed with beauty but cursed with unsuitability. These designs have an attractive autumnal quality because of Georgiadis' frequent use of heavy oranges and browns in his color scheme. The setting for the Snowflakes' Waltz—a sloping terrace adorned with baroque statuary—has been especially admired. Less successful for some balletgoers is the Stahlbaums' house which is not only palatial in scale but, because of Georgiadis' fondness for ochre, black and gold, somewhat somber in appearance; while nineteenth-century homes could be soberly decorated, this one seems far too grand for the Stahlbaums. Still other balletgoers have accused Georgiadis' transformations from one scene to another of being slow and cumbersome—no minor failing in a ballet that depends upon scenic conjuring tricks.

After complaining about how often designers have failed to work magic in *The Nutcracker*, Peter Williams singled out one artist for his conspicuous success in designing the ballet: Alexandre Benois. Benois, said Williams, 'succeeded because he understood completely the child's mind and because he remembered the sensations of a child's Christmas. He also knew how a child would see an adventure in its own kind of two-pence-colored way.' Although Benois designed *The Nutcracker* several times, it is perhaps the Festival Ballet production of 1957 for which he is best known. Admirers of these designs thought that the first-act party had the quaint charm of a Victorian Christmas card, while the second-act settings emphasized the idea of candy implicit in the original scenario. Benois made the Sugarplum Fairy reside in a palace of fudge with sugar icing that had pillars and arches surmounted by jellies and a Christmas pudding.

Another production that makes every architectural element in the Sugarplum Fairy's palace some sort of candy or sweet is that designed by Rouben Ter-Arutunian for the New York City Ballet in 1964. But Ter-Arutunian's candy palace is so immense that there have been balletgoers who have claimed to feel slightly queasy in the stomach just by looking at it.

Left
The Dance of the Mirlitons in Act II. In the 1957 London Festival production David Lichine made the *mirlitons* marzipan shepherdesses.
Above right
This Cincinnati Ballet Company production is set in nineteenth-century Cincinnati and the costumes are modelled on period clothing.
Right
The Snow Queen and her prince in the Land of Snow in the Cincinnati Ballet Company's 1974 production.

Terry Hayworth as
Drosselmeyer and
Manelle Jaye as Clara
watch the children from
the Arts Educational
School in the Chinese
Dance (London Festival
Ballet).

Far left
The Russian Dance from the *divertissements* in a London Festival Ballet production.
Above
A scene from Candyland in the 1975 Ballet West production.
Left
The Chinese Dance in Act II of the 1976 Ballet West production.

Left
After the clock strikes midnight the Christmas tree lights up and the mice and toy soldiers come to life magically (Cincinnati Ballet Company).
Right
The Sugarplum Fairy and her cavalier in the *grand pas de deux* before Clara's departure from the Kingdom of Sweets in a San Jose Dance Theater production.
Below
The Finale from the Ballet West production.

A popular touch in an earlier *Nutcracker* by Benois—that for La Scala in 1938—was a sleigh drawn by polar bears that bore Clara to the Land of Sweets. Benois is not the only designer to incorporate lovable bears into *The Nutcracker*. One of Drosselmeyer's mechanical dolls in the 1954 production by Leonard Weisgard for the San Francisco Ballet was a waddling Russian bear, and the current production by Scottish Ballet, designed by Philip Prowse, gives the Snow Queen two amiable polar bears as attendants.

Leonard Weisgard was an illustrator of children's books and his designs recalled pages out of a child's storybook. Other designers have, like Benois, derived inspiration from old Christmas cards. The front curtain for Rouben Ter-Arutunian's New York City Ballet production depicts an angel and the Christmas star above the snow-covered roofs of a small town. The scene could easily adorn a greeting card. At the end of the second act Clara leaves for home in a reindeer-pulled sleigh—an image familiar from countless greeting cards, as well as from stories and poems about Santa Claus and his sleigh and reindeer.

The fact that that sleigh is able to fly upward into the sky serves as a reminder that *The Nutcracker* provides designers with opportunities for all sorts of wizardry and tricks. The technical crews of ballet companies have been known to refuse to divulge the explanations for the special effects in

their productions, just as professional magicians never tell others the secrets of their tricks. Typically the production stage manager of the Boston Ballet is sworn to silence and keeps the logistics of the staging's spectacular devices a closely guarded secret.

Most often a version's examples of theatrical prestidigitation occur in Clara's dream and indicate the distinction between fantasy and reality. The snow scene is one that permits numerous effects. In the production that Harry Cordwell designed for the London Ballet in 1962, the Snow Queen was first observed frozen inside an iceberg from which she later emerged. Most stagings that include the snow scene make some attempt to provide an illusion of falling snow, usually by means of small objects that are dropped down upon the stage during the course of the dance. Benois's Festival Ballet production simulated snow by means of 750,000 tiny pieces of nylon that were thrown into fans so that they would seem to swirl in the wintry wind as they fell. The Boston Ballet's 'snow' consists of almost a ton of white confetti dropped at each performance.

Other effects can range from the simple to the elaborate. In the Boston Ballet *Nutcracker*, as in certain others, Drosselmeyer appears in a puff of smoke. Ter-Arutunian's effects for the New York City Ballet are so complex that they require a quarter of a million watts of lighting. The most frequently employed special effect in *Nut-*

*cracker*s around the world is a magical Christmas tree that, during Clara's dream, gradually grows and grows until it attains immense proportions. The Boston Ballet's Christmas tree grows to a height of 40 feet on stage, as does the Christmas tree designed by Ter-Arutunian for the New York City Ballet. That tree emerges out of a trapdoor. Because the opening of the trapdoor is visible from various locations in the auditorium, some *Nutcracker* connoisseurs consider Ter-Arutunian's tree less spectacular than the one designed by Horace Armistead for the New York City Ballet's first production of *The Nutcracker* back in 1954. Armistead's tree, though it became nine feet wide, attained a height of only 21 feet and did so by unfolding outward in a strange accordion-like fashion that mystified as well as amazed audiences.

Costume designs by Nicholas Georgiadis for Act I of the Royal Ballet: for a guest (*left*), for a soldier (*center*) and for a boy (*right*).

Usually designers set *The Nutcracker* in a German town that could conceivably be Nuremberg although there is no literal attempt to duplicate Nuremberg's architecture. A few designers have followed their own fancies. For Ballet International in 1976 Peter Farmer removed the first act from town to a farmhouse decorated in the Biedermeier fashion. His second act was also bucolic, taking place in a bower of flowers. In 1956 James Bailey transplanted the action out of Germany entirely for La Scala. Instead he set *The Nutcracker* in Imperial Russia, modelling all his scenes upon elements of the arts, crafts, architecture, and interior decoration associated with St Petersburg. His snow scene was inspired by the designs of the Imperial landscape gardener, Linderhoff, while his Kingdom of Sweets could have

been the creation of the court jeweler, Fabergé.

A few American productions have taken *The Nutcracker* to the New World. Stephen C Wathen, designer for the San Jose Dance Theater version, set the ballet in New England. A particularly ingenious scenic reinterpretation is that of set designer Jay Depenbrock and costumier Anne Peacock Warner for the Cincinnati Ballet. Because Cincinnati is a city that was settled by German immigrants, Depenbrock and Warner have chosen to have their *Nutcracker* occur in the Cincinnati of the 1890s. The costumes are based upon actual clothes that were sold by local department stores at the turn of the century and which are now in the collection of the Cincinnati Historical Society. The Stahlbaums' parlor is largely modelled upon that of an old house owned by Depenbrock's great-aunt. The stained glass window in that parlor, however, is one of the features of the room that does not come from the Depenbrock residence. Instead it is a copy of a stained glass window in Grammer's, one of Cincinnati's old German restaurants.

There are also designers who place *The Nutcracker*—or at least some scenes of it—in a never-never land so fantastic and so remote from ordinary reality that the designs verge upon the nonrepresentational. Thus the snow scene designed by Danish painter Björn Wiinblad for the Royal Danish Ballet in 1971 was not a traditional pine forest but a huge abstraction that reminded critic John Percival of 'a purple sun setting in a yellow sky.'

Of the designs for the idiosyncratic *Nutcracker*s that have nothing to do with Christmas, those of Jürgen Rose for John Neumeier's Royal Winnipeg Ballet version have attracted much favorable comment. No matter what one thinks of Neumeier's approach to the ballet, Rose's designs must be considered an appropriate scenic realization of Neumeier's concepts. The setting for the house reflects the dual forces of coziness and mystery that dominate the ballet. Even details in superficially innocuous pieces of furniture emphasize these themes: thus the overhanging frame of a grim antique couch

Left
The Spanish Dance from
the 1937 Vic-Wells
Ballet production.
Below left
Svetlana Beriosova and
Robert Lunnon as the
Snow Queen and King
in the 1951 Sadler's
Wells Ballet Theatre
production.
Right
The Sugarplum Fairy's
palace designed by
Rouben Ter-Arutunian
for the New York City
Ballet.
Below
Elaine Fifield as the
Sugarplum Fairy of the
1951 Sadler's Wells
Ballet Theatre
production.

has an inset painting of a stormy scene on the moors. Rose also tries to stress Neumeier's theme of growing up by having, among the portraits that are scattered about the room, a painting of Louise in a ballet costume and several others showing her at various times in her life from infancy to womanhood. When the action changes to the local court theater, Rose provides designs for a charmingly ornate Victorian playhouse, all scarlet and gold. The backstage scenes have reminded more than one viewer of the paintings of Degas.

The problems of designing *The Nutcracker* in traditional or unconventional versions have remained largely the same over the past 80 years. The solutions, however, have differed markedly according to the whim of designers, the requirements of choreographers, and the aesthetic tastes of audiences. It is impossible to predict in advance of new productions which otherwise talented artists will fail miserably at their assignments and which will succeed brilliantly beyond anyone's expectations. As Peter Williams has said, 'It is only a very special mind that can design *The Nutcracker*.'

The 'Land of Sweets'

*T*he Nutcracker is a ballet filled with delectables. The guests at the first-act party are surely enjoying holiday treats, and the second act takes place in the Land of Sweets and its *divertissements* refer to good things to eat and drink. Some of the specific things to eat and drink that Petipa, Ivanov, and Tchaikovsky chose to depict in the ballet may seem strange choices to twentieth-century audiences, but they may not have seemed as strange to audiences of the past century, particularly to Russian audiences.

While it is obvious why tea should be represented by a Chinese dance, it is not so obvious why tea should be in the *divertissements* at all, since, except for coffee, the other *divertissements* are tributes to far sweeter things. Yet in the past tea was often used to flavor creams and confections—a use of tea that has fallen so far out of favor that references to it are seldom found even in cookbooks. Today we encounter tea only as a beverage, and one which, moreover, is considered primarily an adult beverage. Parents

Clara and the Nutcracker Prince leave Candyland in a reindeer-drawn sleigh (NYCB).

in the nineteenth century thought otherwise, however, considering tea a perfectly suitable drink for children.

Russians use a samovar for tea brewing and serving. The samovar is merely an urn through which a pipe runs. A coal or charcoal fire is started in the bottom of this pipe and the urn is filled with water. When the water boils, a tea pot is filled with tea and some of the boiling water. This tea is allowed to become very strong, making it almost a tea essence. When the tea is served, the hostess fills her guests' glasses—glasses, not cups, are the traditional receptacles for tea in Russia—partly with the tea extract from the pot and the rest with hot water from the urn, each glass being poured to the taste of the drinker. Usually lemon and sugar are served with the tea, although many Russians are fond of using jam for sweetening. Some Russians also drink their tea while holding a sugar lump between their teeth.

Readers curious about the old use of tea as a flavoring agent might be interested in trying the following recipe.

Right
Clara and the Nutcracker Prince watch the Spanish dancers in a New York City Ballet production.
Far right
Little cooks in the Kingdom of Sweets prepare for the arrival of Clara and the Nutcracker (London Festival Ballet).
Below
Chinese dancer from Act II of a Ballet West production.

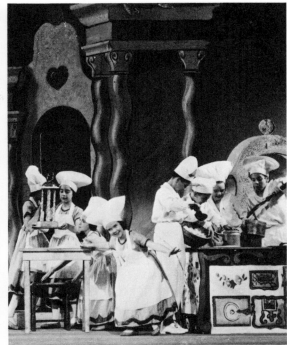

Tea-Flavored Custard Cream

Beat in the top of a double boiler:
   6 egg yolks
   1 cup sugar
   1 teaspoon cornstarch
until the mixture forms ribbons when the whisk is raised from the pot. Moisten it gradually with
   $2\frac{1}{2}$ cups milk infused with
   2 teaspoons tea
To infuse milk: mix milk and tea in a heavy pan. Scald them together and strain the milk while still hot.
Cook the mixture over hot water until it can coat a metal spoon with a thick layer of custard. Chill.

Chocolate in *The Nutcracker* is represented by Spanish dancers—and quite rightly so, because chocolate, which comes from Mexico, was introduced to Europe in 1519 by Spaniards following their conquest of the New World. Its use spread rapidly across the continent, and in the seventeenth century 'chocolate houses' almost replaced the already common 'coffee houses,' since the drinking of chocolate had become very fashionable. Hot chocolate eventually went out of fashion, leaving coffee to reign as the universal drink of Western Europe.

Though it never replaced tea as the universal drink for millions of Russians, chocolate was nevertheless enjoyed in Russia, where it was introduced during the time of Peter the Great (1672–1725). Usually it was given to children as a hot beverage for breakfast, and if one imagines that Clara (despite the fact that the scenario says she is supposed to be a little German girl) was raised in the same way as the little Russian girls in the audience at the Maryinsky, then it was as a beverage, rather than in the form of candy, that she probably first encountered chocolate. Hot chocolate is still very popular in France, where special mugs are designed specifically for its consumption.

Here is a recipe for

Hot Chocolate

For the preparation of chocolate as a drink, per cup use
   1 generous ounce of sweet chocolate
   ¼ cup rich milk

Heat over very low flame until the chocolate softens and is fairly melted. Remove from the heat and whip into a smooth paste. Add
   1 cup scalding milk
per serving, adding it a little bit at a time, incorporating it well after each addition. Chocolate should never be allowed to boil, as that robs it of some of its aroma and gives the milk an unpleasant taste. Brillat-Savarin gives the following secret for increasing the flavor of hot chocolate: 'When you want to taste good chocolate, make it the night before in a faïence coffee pot, and leave it. The chocolate becomes concentrated during the night and this gives it a much better consistency.'

Although *mirlitons* are flutes, the figures who dance to their piping in many productions of *The Nutcracker* are said to be made of marzipan. First produced by nuns, marzipan is one of the great triumphs of the French confectionery art. Essentially it is a mixture of almonds, sugar, egg whites, and bitter almonds (or almond extract, since the sale of bitter almonds is prohibited in the United States without a doctor's prescription). In Russia during the nineteenth century marzipan was worked with extra egg whites and candied orange peel, resulting in what the French termed *Massepain à la Russe*. Clara undoubtedly ate these confections at Christmas as a treat. Since they contained flour, they more closely resembled cookies than they did candies. None the less, they are delicious.

Right
Antoinette Sibley in Act II of a Royal Ballet production.
Below
Manola Asensio as the Snow Fairy in the Land of Ice and Snow (London Festival Ballet).
Bottom
The Spanish Dance from a Royal Ballet production.

Massepain à la Russe

Mix in a medium bowl:
  ¾ cup flour
  2 tablespoons cornstarch or potato flour
  2¾ cups fine sugar
Add two at a time:
  8 egg whites
beating well after each addition
Thoroughly incorporate:
  ¾ lb (12 oz) ground almonds (NB)
  ½ lb (8 oz) finely chopped candied orange peel
Pipe the paste on to buttered and floured baking sheets, using a large star or other decorative tip. The massepains should be an inch and a half across at most. Bake in a 400 degree oven for 12–15 minutes, or until brown only around the edges. Remove them from the sheet while they are still hot.

Above
Boston Ballet principal dancers Laura Young and Woytek Lowski as the Sugarplum Fairy and her cavalier.
Left
Fernando Bujones, Nathalia Makarova and Alexandre Minsk in the American Ballet Theater production.

(NB—To grind almonds easily, first blanch them. Next, place them in the container of a blender or food processor, using about 3 tablespoons of sugar to prevent them from becoming paste. Process them until no large pieces are seen. Sieving the finished product is not necessary.)

Possibly the most famous character in all of *The Nutcracker* is the Sugarplum Fairy, yet many twentieth-century children probably do not know what a sugarplum is and they probably have never eaten one, although sugarplums have been around since the beginning of the seventeenth century. A sugarplum is really nothing more than a small round or oval sweetmeat made of boiled

bottom of the container. Pour off the liquid carefully so the sediment is not included.

Measure the liquid. For each cup of liquid poured into a very large pot, measure and add:

$2\frac{1}{2}$ cups sugar

Bring to a boil, stirring to combine the ingredients. Skim off any foam that may rise to the surface; otherwise, the entire batch may be grainy. Cook to the hard crack stage (310 degrees F), being careful that the mixture does not caramelize. Remove pan from heat and when it stops bubbling add colorings and flavorings to taste. It is usually colored pink or pastel green and left unflavored, though it lends itself well to vanilla or peppermint. Pour the candy onto an oiled marble slab or metal sheet. When it begins to cool and a hard 'skin' forms on the surface, mark it into squares, lozenges, strips, or rounds. Strips are traditional and are usually twisted while still warm; allow other shapes to cool completely before breaking.

Other variations have appeared in Europe and America, many having as their basis dates or dried figs and raisins. Some are even a variation of marzipan or some other candy. Thus sugarplum has come to be a generic rather than a specific term for a sweet.

sugar, variously colored and flavored, but there have been innumerable variations upon sugarplums over the past three centuries. Usually, however, barley sugar has been employed as the basic ingredient.

Barley Sugar

Cook together for 5 hours:
  1 cup pearled barley
  5 quarts water
Strain the rather gelatinous liquid through several thicknesses of cheesecloth into a large jar or bowl. Allow to sit undisturbed for 3 or 4 hours in order to collect any remaining sediment at the

Balletgoers possessing both a sweet tooth and a love of dance history might find it interesting to learn that Tchaikovsky was not the only well-known composer to write a ballet filled with edibles and drinkables. Indeed the sweets of *The Nutcracker* pale in comparison with the glutton's feast of foodstuffs in *Schlagobers*, a ballet with music by

Below
Colleen Neary and Peter Martins (New York City Ballet).
Right
Antoinette Sibley and Anthony Dowell (Royal Ballet).

Richard Strauss and choreography by Heinrich Kröller, produced by the Vienna State Opera Ballet on 9 May 1924. Taking its title from a type of cream-filled Viennese pastry, *Schlagobers* consists of the visions of a little boy who has been taken to a confectioner's shop as a confirmation day present.

The confections, of course, come alive, and among the participants in the *divertissements* that follow are Princess Teaflower,

Prince Coffee, Prince Cocoa, Don Sugaro, and Princess Praline, accompanied by Christmas crackers, chocolate sausages, gingerbread, marzipan, sugarplum soldiers, a chorus of sponge cakes, roly-polies, plum cakes, pretzels, éclairs, gingersnaps, wafers, Turkish delight, and a *corps de ballet* of whipped cream. There are also variations for dancers representing Chartreuse, Slivovitz, and Vodka—even though these would seem quite unsuitable beverages to appear in a child's dream. Tension mounts when the pastries attempt to riot and revolt, and their tumult is quelled only when tea, coffee, and cocoa have been poured upon the rioters. Santa Claus arrives during the victory festivities, and at the ballet's conclusion everyone is happy—except, perhaps, those ballet lovers who have come down with choreographic indigestion.

Productions on the Screen

In 1940, the same year in which the Ballet Russe de Monte Carlo introduced *The Nutcracker* on the stage to America, there was another version of *The Nutcracker* that ultimately did much to popularize Tchaikovsky's music. Though it could in a sense be termed choreographic, and though it was certainly scenically spectacular, this version was not in the least balletic. Rather, it was cinematic, for excerpts from the Nutcracker Suite were used in *Fantasia*, Walt Disney's animated film based upon famous pieces of classical music.

It is said that part of the inspiration for *Fantasia* came from the distinguished conductor, Leopold Stokowski, who met Walt Disney one day at a Hollywood party. When Stokowski, an admirer of Disney's cartoons, told the film-maker that he would like to work with him sometime, Disney confessed that he had an idea for a musical cartoon. Earlier in his career Disney had won praise for his series of 'Silly Symphonies,' in which the movements of cartoon characters were wittily synchronized with musical rhythms. Now Disney was thinking of another cartoon

Mikhail Baryshnikov and Marianna Tcherkassky in the American Ballet Theater production.

in a similar vein, this one employing actual symphonic music. Disney had heard Paul Dukas' tone poem, *The Sorcerer's Apprentice*, based upon an old legend that has attracted the attention of many writers and artists, among them Goethe. The legend concerns a boy apprenticed to a sorcerer, who is forced to do menial housework for his master, the most laborious of his chores being that of carrying water from the well. When the sorcerer goes away on an errand, the boy steals his magic hat and makes a broom come to life to do the water-carrying for him. After setting the broom into motion, the apprentice discovers that he does not know how to make the broom stop.

Disney thought this story and Dukas' music could form the basis for a pleasant cartoon starring Mickey Mouse as the apprentice. Stokowski was delighted by the notion and agreed to conduct the score should Disney ever produce the film. But then he wondered, why stop there? Why not make an entire feature-length film using concert music? Emboldened by the conductor's encouragement, Disney went to work on *Fantasia*. The staff of the Disney studios listened to hundreds of pieces of music before settling upon those used in the movie. By 1939 Stokowski had started recording with the Philadelphia Orchestra.

The film was unusual in many ways, most of all because of its combination of 'popular' entertainment and 'highbrow' art. Another novelty of the film was its total absence of written screen credits. Instead there was spoken commentary by the music critic, Deems Taylor. *Fantasia* has always been controversial. For one thing, Stokowski, although a magnificent conductor at his best, could play 'fast and loose' with music, rearranging and reorchestrating pieces as his fancy moved him. He abridged and touched up several of the pieces in *Fantasia* and so extensively rearranged *The Rite of Spring* that its composer, Igor Stravinsky, was horrified at the results.

Film critics consider *Fantasia* undeniably fascinating, but also uneven as a visual spec-

Mikhail Baryshnikov and Marianna Tcherkassky (American Ballet Theater).

194

tacle. Apparently everyone approves of *The Sorcerer's Apprentice*, starring Mickey Mouse. Almost equally popular is the transformation of the Dance of the Hours from Ponchielli's opera, *La Gioconda* into a farcical ballet for an ensemble of ostriches, elephants, crocodiles, and hippos. Persons unfamiliar with dance history enjoy its absurdities, while the knowledgeable relish it as a satire upon the worst clichés of classical ballet. Certain critics have also had kind words for the semi-abstract images that accompany Bach's Toccata and Fugue in D Minor, calling the sequence an attempt to mix 'absolute' music and 'non-representational' art.

At his worst Disney could be guilty of excess. And several critics have charged various scenes in *Fantasia* with being excessive indeed. Some object to turning *The Rite of Spring* into a cartoon view of prehistory, complete with belching volcanos and battling dinosaurs. Others object to the sentimental interpretation of Beethoven's Sixth Symphony. That symphony may be subtitled *Pastoral* and it may be an idealization of a day in the country, but Disney's romanticized idyll, complete with cuddly cherubs and whimsically caricatured Greek gods and centaurs (including such mythological peculiarities as lady centaurs) has struck viewers as being unnecessarily coy.

The excerpts from the Nutcracker Suite represent Disney at his best and worst. To the variation for the Sugarplum Fairy, sprites flit among flowers and make them sparkle with dew. If this scene verges upon the sacharine, the next is charming, for it turns the Chinese Dance into a dance for mushrooms, whose mushroom caps resemble coolie hats. Flowers float on stream water to the music for the Mirlitons and their spinnings recall the complicated chorus girl formations of the Hollywood musicals choreographed by Busby Berkeley. The Arabian Dance has been set underwater and the undulations of fish and aquatic plants harmonize surprisingly well with the languor of the music. Some viewers may be disappointed that Disney has introduced an obvious joke here: the fish wink seductively with heavily lidded eyes, as though they were finny Mae Wests.

Above and left
Scenes from the American Ballet Theater.

The Trepak, however, is another charmer, for it is conceived as a dance for bounding thistles that bear a faint resemblance to Cossacks. Celebrating the changing of the seasons, Disney's Waltz of the Flowers features fairies who turn summer leaves to autumn brown. The scene concludes with the arrival of winter frosts.

When *Fantasia* was released in 1940, there were those who considered it peculiar, for it lost money. Over the years, however, its fame has increased and in the hippie era of the 1960s it achieved a reputation as a filmic 'high' or cinematic 'trip.' Despite the objections of film and music critics, *Fantasia* appears to gain popularity each time it is revived. In so doing it has also helped to make Tchaikovsky's Nutcracker Suite one of America's most familiar pieces of classical music.

Curiously enough, although the fantasy of *The Nutcracker* would seem a natural for cinematic treatment, almost no one other than Disney has done much to present the ballet in the movies or on television. Balanchine's New York City Ballet production, John Neumeier's Canadian *Nutcracker*, and Willam Christensen's Ballet West version are among those that have been televised. In 1960 Martha Myers's 'A Time to Dance' series of dance appreciation television programs included a performance of *The Nutcracker pas de deux* by Melissa Hayden and

Jacques d'Amboise. Film catalogues also list a Waltz of the Flowers by the Bolshoi Ballet in a Soviet movie called *Ballet Concert*, a *Nutcracker pas de deux* by Mary Ellen Moylan and Oleg Tupine of the Ballet Russe, and a Sugarplum Fairy solo by Alicia Markova, as performed at the Jacob's Pillow Dance Festival.

In 1965 Warner Brothers made a *Nutcracker* film in Germany choreographed by Kurt Jacob. The music was played by the Budapest Symphony Orchestra, the great

George de la Pena and Roman Jasinsky in the Russian Dance for the American Ballet Theater.

German modern dancer Harald Kreutzberg was Drosselmeyer, and the international case of dancers included Melissa Hayden, Patricia McBride, Edward Villella, Ray Barra, and Hugo Dellavalle. Also in the film were Helga Heinrich and Niels Kehlet, who interpolated the Bluebird *pas de deux* from *The Sleeping Beauty* into *The Nutcracker*. Despite the illustrious cast, the film has been cooly received by critics, although it sometimes turns up on American educational television stations as a Christmas special.

Despite Disney's uncertainties in taste, *Fantasia* still remains the most successful attempt to bring *The Nutcracker* to the screen.

The Significance of the Nutcracker

Choreographers often add to one part of the ballet and subtract from another, and they emphasize this or that detail or invent a completely new sequence where something else used to happen in *The Nutcracker*. This is one reason why it is so interesting to compare versions of the ballet. However, should choreographers introduce too many changes into a production, they may end up with a *Nutcracker* which bears only a fleeting resemblance to the traditional scenario. Some choreographers have been more than willing to take such risks—indeed, they have been challenged and stimulated by them—and, as a result, there have been *Nutcracker* productions (some welcomed with applause, others receiving only gapes of disbelief) that might be termed idiosyncratic or even downright eccentric.

What in some ways may be considered the oddest *Nutcracker* production of all times was premiered by Les Ballets Trockadero de Monte Carlo on 19 December 1974 at the Touchstone Theater in New York City. Choreographed by Tamara Karpova (who also danced the Sugarplum Fairy), it was a version similar to that of the old Ballet Russe de Monte Carlo, presenting both acts but

The Pastorale of Act II from a production by the Royal Ballet.

divertissements are light and airy, and choreographers often fill them with leaps and lifts. Dramatically the first act presents emotion after emotion in quick succession as a friendly party gives way to a nightmarish battle with mice. The battle in turn is followed by a magical journey to a never-never land. Once Clara has arrived in the Sugarplum Fairy's realm, dramatic suspense vanishes. Instead of constant changes of moods and feelings, there is a suite of *divertissements* in which each dance expresses, in its own leisurely way, a single mood or feeling. Skeptics may pronounce Petipa's scenario intellectually trivial, yet the way it permits so many different kinds of things to happen on stage keeps the eye interested.

The ear is also interested. *The Nutcracker* is blessed with a fine score. Indeed if it were not for Tchaikovsky's music, *The Nutcracker* might no longer be staged, given the objections that have been raised against the deficiencies of the story and the original choreography. But everyone, or almost everyone, likes Tchaikovsky's music and, from the earliest days of recordings, orchestras and record companies have loved to record it. As Pittman Corry, Director of Atlanta's Southern Ballet, has said, 'Our pioneer orchestras (the Boston and Philadelphia primarily) did a marvelous saturation job on the public as far as *Nuts* is concerned. Music from this ballet, as recorded by one of those orchestras, was the first classical record I ever heard. One almost grew up with the music.'

In some ways *The Nutcracker* is so constructed that it can be adapted to fit almost any sort of ballet company. There are a few inherent limitations, of course. *The Nutcracker* cannot be performed by a mere handful of dancers; excerpts from the work (the *pas de deux* or a few of the *divertissements*) may conceivably be presented on a small scale, but not the complete ballet: *The Nutcracker* is not choreographic chamber music. Nevertheless *The Nutcracker* is surprisingly flexible and resilient, inviting all sorts of interpretations by all sorts of dancers and choreographers—perhaps partly why it is so popular with American regional ballet companies.

Gelsey Kirkland (*left*) and Nathalia Makarova as Clara in productions by the American Ballet Theater.

There are roles for everybody. Well-trained dancers can sparkle in the *divertissements*. Children can be seen in parts which do not overtax their technical abilities but which make them look alert and charming on stage. It seldom takes much persuasion to get parents with dreams of theatrical glory to play the adults at the first-act party. Consequently the casts of community *Nutcracker* productions may contain local businessmen, clergymen, physicians, and lawyers. The role of Drosselmeyer is sometimes given to someone particularly prominent in town— to the mayor, perhaps, or a college president. The Drosselmeyer in the 1977 production of *The Nutcracker* by the Connecticut Ballet of New Haven was Angelo Bartlett Giamatti, who that year became the eighteenth president of Yale University. If a company likes to import guest stars, *The Nutcracker* is an especially good vehicle for them because, having little to do other than a spectacular

pas de deux which is a complete unit in itself, they can arrive late in the schedule of rehearsals and still be easily fitted into the production.

Nevertheless practical production matters alone cannot explain why 'Nothing quite

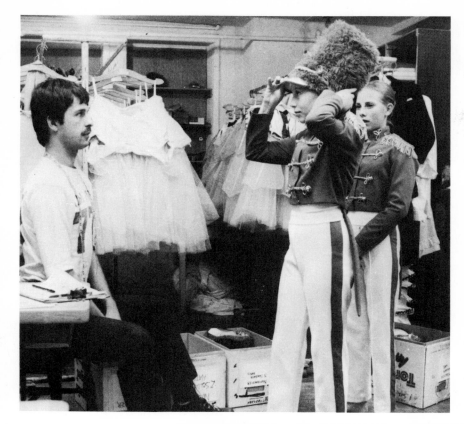

catches the heart as *The Nutcracker* does at Christmas!'—as Moscelyne Larkin, Co-director of the Tulsa Ballet, once exclaimed. Nor does its variety of roles for dancers of divergent technical levels explain why, for the dancer friends of American critic George Dorris, 'Christmas Eve isn't official until we have played *The Nutcracker*, all of it—sometimes twice.' What is the secret of *The Nutcracker*?

There are those *Nutcracker* lovers who fear that even asking such a question might dissipate some of the magic. These commentators would recommend just sitting back and letting the ballet cast its spell. 'In such works as this,' A H Franks recommends, 'let us not search for significance and serious attempt at characterization, but participate vicariously in the joyousness, the humor, and the rich fabric of the entire spectacle.' Too much analysis, perhaps, might spoil *The Nutcracker*.

Above
Fitting the costumes in preparation for a production by Ballet West.
Right
Battle of the mice and toy soldiers in a London Festival Ballet production.
Left above and below
Rehearsing for the Ballet West *Nutcracker*.

Not necessarily, reply another group of balletgoers. True, they say, *The Nutcracker* should not be inflicted with pedantic obfuscation. But because they believe, along with Edwin Denby, that 'The Nutcracker' is not foolish in form, nor is it foolish either in its literal content,' so they maintain that a sympathetic analysis of the ballet may bring rewards.

The focus and the terms of any such analysis are apt to change, depending upon the temperament of the commentator and the cultural and political circumstances of the time in which he lives. In times of unrest it is particularly tempting to stress the domestic coziness of the first act. Lincoln Kirstein, Director of the New York City Ballet, believes that it is absolutely essential for that act to convey the feeling of a comfortable middle-class household, for its domesticity constitutes the norm against which all the other events of the ballet are measured. Because the Stahlbaums' household comes to seem so comfortably familiar, the magical scenes that follow seem all the more surprising, since the familiar has now been invaded by the strange.

But the strangeness of *The Nutcracker* is neither malign nor threatening—at least once the mice are vanquished. Rather, *The Nutcracker* transports the viewer to a kind of dream world—a utopia of a sort—in which there are no headaches, heartaches, or stomachaches. During the 1950s when the tensions of the Cold War dominated international politics, the benign escapism of *The Nutcracker* must have seemed especially appealing. Shortly after the New York City

Nathalia Makarova and Alexandre Minsk in Act I of the American Ballet Theater production.

Ballet premiered its *Nutcracker* in 1954, Anatole Chujoy wrote, 'At a time when the whole world seems on the verge of falling apart, at a time when nearly every facet of our life is being reduced to a state of primitivism, from which one can hardly see a return to a higher civilization, Balanchine's creation of a classic ballet, in all its well-ordered values, is a reason for hope and joy.' Chujoy then listed the qualities of classicism present in *The Nutcracker* as 'lucidity, simplicity, dignity, and correctness of style.'

A number of commentators have stressed the idyllic vision of childhood that *The Nutcracker* presents. George Dorris has pointed out that in his three ballet scores Tchaikovsky composed 'a kind of cycle dealing with important aspects of man's life. *The Nutcracker* presents childhood with its joys, disappointments, mystery, and enchantment. *The Sleeping Beauty*, which begins with birth, primarily shows youth and young love, the necessity of learning good manners, magnanimity, and a sense of proportion if one is to live with others. *Swan Lake*, starting with coming to adulthood, mainly concentrates on the relation between love and death.' This cycle of three ballets, Dorris realizes, was quite unintentional on Tchaikovsky's part, 'for the subjects of at least two were presented to him, and they were composed in the reverse order to that which

Antoinette Sibley and Anthony Dowell in the *pas de deux* of Act II in a Royal Ballet production.

Final scene from a Bolshoi Ballet production.

George Balanchine also believes that *The Nutcracker* concerns childhood, but his emphasis is somewhat different from that of Asafiev. Balanchine contends that the ballet celebrates the powers of human imagination, powers that children possess in abundance, but which adults often allow to wither away under the pressures of ordinary everyday life. Because the imagination can be such a potent force, *The Nutcracker* can be viewed as a potentially subversive ballet. 'Actually, it's not a dream,' says Balanchine of the events in the ballet, 'it's the reality that Mother didn't believe. The story was written by Hoffmann against society. He said that society, the grownups, really have no imagination, and that they try to suppress the imagination of children. In Germany, they were very strict—no nonsense. They didn't understand that nonreality is the real thing.'

Edwin Denby, an American critic famous for his poetic insights into ballets, wrote two essays on *The Nutcracker* a decade apart. The first, 'The Nutcracker 1890 Model Ballet,' was published in 1944 at a time when it was becoming fashionable to interpret works of art in terms of Freudian psychology. To this day no one is quite sure just how far Denby's tongue was in his cheek, but it is generally assumed that he was writing with at least a touch of levity. A few of his notions, however, seem to prefigure some of those that Rudolf Nureyev seriously incorporated into his staging of *The Nutcracker* almost a quarter-century later. In any case Denby in 1944 started off by saying that 'nowadays with psychoanalysis practically a household remedy, grownups take the nonsense of fairy tales more seriously than children. We call them narratives in free association and solve them like crossword puzzles. *The Nutcracker* is an easy one—the title gives it away. The story begins on Christmas Eve in an upper-class home, the *locus classicus* of ambivalent anxiety. An elderly bachelor with one eye gives a pre-adolescent girl a male nutcracker (the symbols and inversion could not be more harrowing). . . . She dreams that the nutcracker turns almost into a boy.' The suite of dances about candy 'presents an intelligible association series, operated with

211

unconscious sexual symbols. . . .' Still *The Nutcracker* succeeds in 'turning envy and pain into lovely invention and social harmony.'

Indeed Denby does have to admit that, whatever it may ultimately mean psychologically, 'What you see on the stage is a suite of well-mannered dances, graceful and clear.' And when Denby wrote another essay called simply '*The Nutcracker*' in 1954, it was the ballet's good manners, grace, and clarity that he stressed. He began by noting that 'A troubled New York poet sighed, "I could see it every day, it's so deliciously boring." The sentiments are those of family life, Christmas Eve, children growing up among adults, a little girl's odd and beautiful imagination. And the miracle is that these familiar sentiments appear on stage without vulgarization or coyness, with brilliant danc-

George de la Pena and Marianna Tcherkassky as the Nutcracker Prince and Clara in the American Ballet Theater production.

212

ing, light fun, and with the amplitude of a
child's wonderful premonitions.'

Among the pleasures of *The Nutcracker*
for Denby was that 'of seeing children on
stage who are not made to look saccharine
or hysterical, who do what they do naturally
and straight.' The ballet also struck him as
a glorification of sociability, conviviality,
and the party spirit. Indeed, he pointed out
that *The Nutcracker* tells the story of two
parties—'of a party at home and then of a
party at the Fairy's house. The agitations of
Christmas Eve lead to a small nightmare, a
nostalgic journey, a glorious arrival. At the
Fairy's there is everything that is best at
home, radiantly clear.' Elaborating upon the
theme of parties, Denby said, 'The leisurely
oppressive pacing of the party is in one sense
the token of a responsible ruling class; but

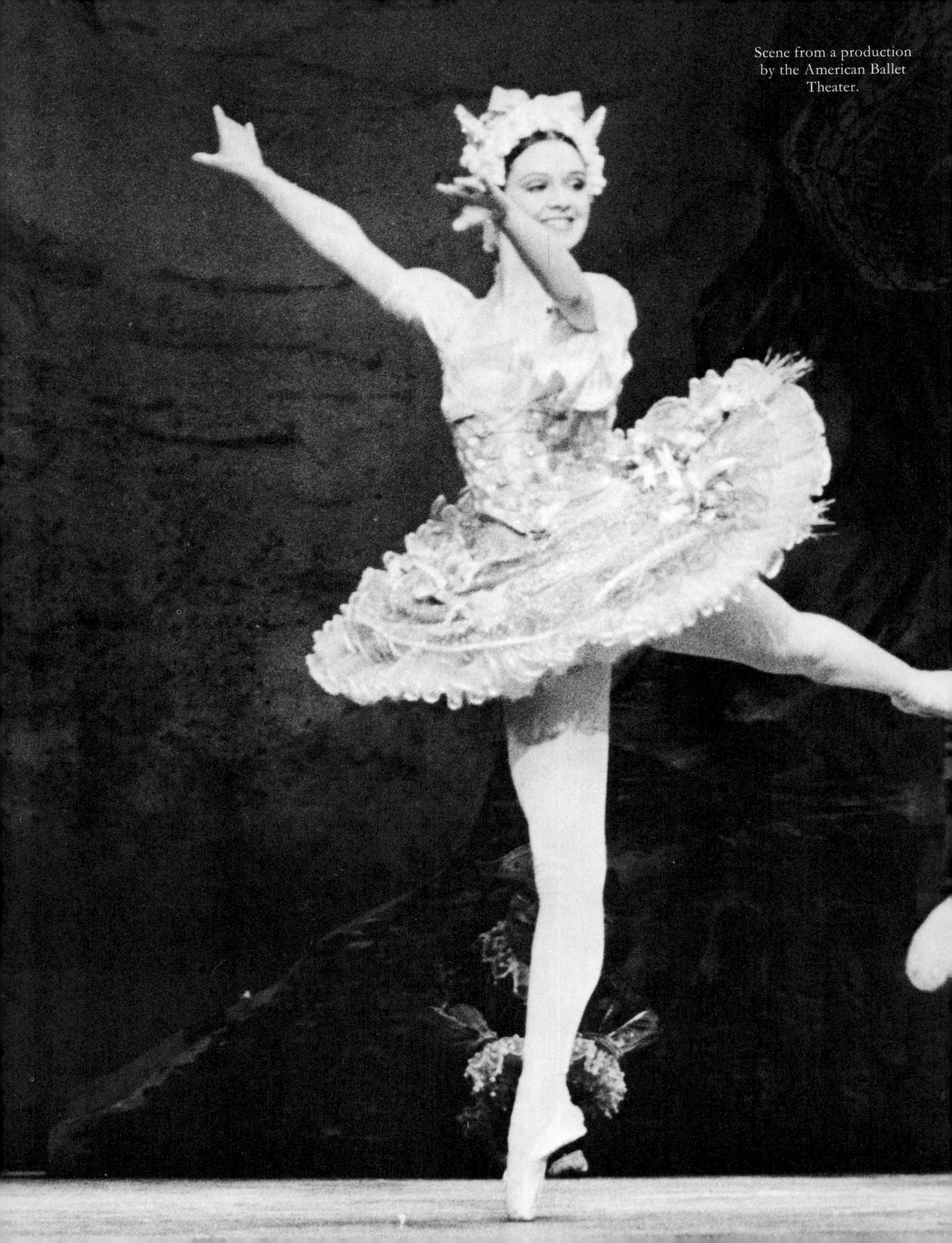

Scene from a production by the American Ballet Theater.

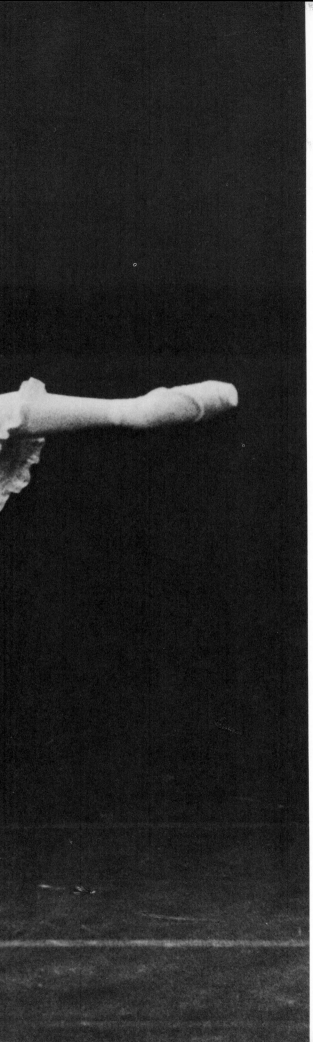

Fernando Bujones and Nathalia Makarova as the Nutcracker Prince and Clara in the production staged by the American Ballet Theater.

in another it creates the large time in which childhood events occur, the amplitude out of which fantasy takes shape. The party unfolds a story of mutual behavior, good manners and bad. . . . All these manners sharpen one's eye for the so-to-speak heavenly manners of the Fairy's palace, the graceful behavior of classic dancing.' *The Nutcracker*, then, is 'the story of a child's presentiment of handsome conduct, of civilized society; it is no foolish subject, and it gives the ballet its secret radiance.'

Denby discovered that grownups watching *The Nutcracker* 'can slip back into a world they have left. The buried longings of it are there glittering still. . . .' The magical world of *The Nutcracker*—the radiant realm of home and family in the first act, the explicitly magical realm of fantasy in the second—is therefore a kind of Eden. Poet W H Auden made a similar observation the basis for an essay on *The Nutcracker* that he titled 'Ballet's Present Eden.'

Auden begins with some aesthetic speculations to the effect that every art form 'has its peculiar nature which allows it to express some things better than any rival medium.' The medium of the ballet, he argues, is movement in space in a unique relationship with time: 'Ballet time, that is, is a continuous present; every experience which depends on historical time lies outside its capacities.' Therefore 'in its dazzling display of physical energy . . . the ballet expresses, as no other medium can, the joy of being alive.' In other words 'all real ballets take place in Eden, in that world of pure being without becoming and the suffering implied by becoming, a world where things, beasts and men are equally alive, a world without history and without seriousness.'

With its vision of family life and its glorification of parties, *The Nutcracker* is a ballet that takes place in a choreographic Eden. It is 'a festival of joy.' And by stating what every lover of *The Nutcracker* has always instinctively known, despite the jeers of skeptics, Auden concludes by declaring that 'only those who have lost their sense of joy and for whom, consequently, ballet is a meaningless art will find that juvenile.'

Bibliography

Above
Patricia McBride and
Edward Villella of the
New York City Ballet.
Below
Mazzo and Ludlow of
the New York City
Ballet.

Abraham, Gerald, ed, *The Music of Tchaikovsky*. New York: W W Norton and Company, Inc, 1946.

Anderson, Jack, "A Bolshoi Portfolio," *Dance Magazine*, June 1966, pp 44-51.

Anderson, Jack, "A New American Tradition," *Dance Magazine*, December 1966, pp 45-55, 68-69.

Auden, W H, "Ballet's Present Eden," *Center: A Magazine of the Performing Arts*, February 1954.

Balanchine, George and Francis Mason, *Balanchine's Complete Stories of the Great Ballets*. Garden City: Doubleday and Company, Inc, 1977.

Barnes, Clive, "Gore's Nutcracker," *Dance and Dancers*, December 1962, pp 26-28.

Barnes, Clive, "New York City Ballet's *Nutcracker*," *Dance and Dancers*, March 1966, pp 17-19.

Barnes, Clive, "The Nutcracker," *Dance and Dancers*, December 1957, pp 11-15.

Barnes, Clive, "The Nutcracker," *Dance and Dancers*, February 1958, pp 14-15.

Beamont, Cyril W, *Complete Book of Ballets*. New York: Grosset and Dunlop, 1938.

Benois, Alexandre, *Reminiscences of the Russian Ballet*, trans by Mary Britnieva. London: Putnam, 1941.

Blom, Eric, *Tchaikovsky Orchestral Works*. Westport: Greenwood Press, 1970.

Buckle, Richard, *Nijinsky*. London: Weidenfeld and Nicolson, 1971.

Carp, Louis, "Small Fry and 'The Nutcracker,'" *Dance Magazine*, December 1957, pp 38-40, 92.

Christout, Marie-Françoise, "Ballets de Marseille Roland Petit," *Dance and Dancers*, March 1977, pp 19-21.

Chujoy, Anatole, "The Nutcracker, Then and Now," *Dance News*, February 1945, pp 8-9.

Chujoy, Anatole, "The Season in Review," *Dance News*, March 1954, p 7.

Clarke, Mary and Clement Crisp, *Making a Ballet*. London: Studio Vista, 1974.

Clarke, Mary, "Nureyev's Nutcracker," *The Dancing Times*, April 1968, pp 346-348.

Clarke, Mary, "The Nutcracker," *The Dancing Times*, February 1958, p 216.

Clarke, Mary, *The Sadler's Wells Ballet*. London: Adam and Charles Black, 1955.

Clarke, Mary, "A Traditional Nutcracker," *The Dancing Times*, February 1976, pp 252-253.

Croce, Arlene, *Afterimages*. New York: Alfred A Knopf, 1977.

Crowle, Pigeon, *The Nutcracker Ballet*. London: Faber and Faber Limited, 1958.

Denby, Edwin, *Dancers, Buildings, and People in the Streets*. New York: Horizon Press, 1965.

Denby, Edwin, *Looking at the Dance*. New York: Horizon Press, 1968.

Dorris, George, "The Legacy of Hurok," *Ballet Review*, Vol V, No 1, pp 78-88.

Dowling, Colette, "NYCB's Children," New York City Ballet Lincoln Center program, 1976.

Drew, David, *The Decca Book of Ballet*. London: Frederick Muller Limited, 1958.

Ehrmann-Ewart, Hans, "News from Latin America," *Dance Magazine*, December 1958, p 122.

Evans, Edwin, *Tchaikovsky*. London: J M Dent, 1935.

Feinstein, Martin, "Tchaikovsky, Swan Lake and the Nutcracker," Bolshoi Ballet souvenir program for 1966 US tour.

Fiske, Roger, *Ballet Music*. London: George G Harrap and Company, 1958.

Franks, A H, *Approach to the Ballet*. London: Sir Isaac Pitman and Sons Ltd, 1948.

Franks, A H, "London Ballet's *Nutcracker*," *The Dancing Times*, November 1962, pp 74-75.

Goodwin, Noel, "Ballet International," *Dance and Dancers*, March 1977, p 21.

Goodwin, Noel, "Nutcracking on the Border," *Dance and Dancers*, February 1974, pp 30-35.

Haskell, Arnold L, *Dancing Round the World*. London: Victor Gollancz Ltd, 1937.

Hering, Doris, "The Foolish Excesses of Yesterday," *Dance Magazine*, July 1966, p 28.

Hoffmann, E T A, *The Best Tales of Hoffmann*, ed, by E F Bleiler. New York: Dover Publications Inc, 1967.

Kerensky, Oleg, *Anna Pavlova*. New York: E P Dutton and Co, Inc, 1973.

Kerensky, Oleg, *Ballet Scene*. London: Hamish Hamilton, 1970.

Kirstein, Lincoln, *Movement and Metaphor*. New York: Praeger Publishers, 1970.

Kirstein, Lincoln, "The Nutcracker," New York City Ballet Lincoln Center program, 1975.

Koegler, Horst, "Lively Winter Season," *Dance and Dancers*, April 1972, pp 51-54.

Lassalle, Nancy, "Some Distinguished Alumni of the Nutcracker," New York City Ballet Lincoln Center program, 1975.

Lawrence, Robert, *The Victor Book of Ballets and Ballet Music*. New York: Simon and Schuster, 1950.

Manchester, P W, "New York Newsletter," *The Dancing Times*, March 1968, pp 305-307.

Marks, Marcia, "Dancing Shoes With Nimble Souls," *Dance Magazine*, July 1968, pp 46-51, 84-86.

Maskey, Jacqueline, "A Dream of Christmas," New York City Ballet Lincoln Center program, 1966.

Maynard, Olga, "The Nutcracker," *Dance Magazine*, December 1973, pp 51-72.

McDonagh, Don, "Face-Saving Season," *Dance and Dancers*, August 1968, pp 38-39.

Monahan, James, "The Nutcracker," Royal Ballet souvenir program for 1968 US tour.

Monahan, James, "The Nutcracker and Other Royal Ballet Activities," *The Dancing Times*, January 1974, pp 210-212.

Monahan, James, "A Parcel of Nutcrackers," *The Dancing Times*, February 1977, pp 260-262.

"'The Nutcracker' Has a Birthday," *Dance Magazine*, December 1967, pp 38-39.

Percival, John, "Revivals and Creations in Copenhagen," *Dance and Dancers*, April 1972, pp 39-43.

Reynolds, Nancy, *Repertory in Review*. New York: The Dial Press, 1977.

Roslavleva, Natalia, *Era of the Russian Ballet*. New York: E P Dutton and Co, Inc, 1966.

Samachson, Dorothy and Joseph, *The Russian Ballet and Three of Its Masterpieces*. New York: Lothrop, Lee and Shepard Company, 1971.

Siegel, Marcia B, *Watching the Dance Go By*. Boston: Houghton Mifflin Company, 1977.

Terry, Walter, *Ballet: A New Guide to the Liveliest Art*. New York: Dell Publishing Co, Inc, 1959.

Tobias, Tobi, "Celebration," *Dance Magazine*, December 1977, pp 51-52.

Vaughan, David, *Frederick Ashton and His Ballets*. New York: Alfred A Knopf, 1977.

Weinstock, Herbert, *Tchaikovsky*. New York: Alfred A Knopf, 1966.

Williams, Peter, "Gore's Nutcracker: Decor," *Dance and Dancers*, December 1962, pp 28-30.

Williams, Peter, "Hard Nut," *Dance and Dancers*, April 1968, pp 13-19.

Williams, Peter, "London Festival Ballet," *Dance and Dancers*, March 1977, pp 21-24.

Williams, Peter, "The Nutcracker: Decor," *Dance and Dancers*, February 1958, pp 15-17.

Williams, Peter, "Nutcracking in Two Cities: London Festival Ballet's *The Nutcracker*," *Dance and Dancers*, March 1966, pp 12-14.

Wilson, G B L, "Zurich Ballet," *The Dancing Times*, February 1970, p 242.

Above
Melissa Hayden and Jacques d'Amboise of the New York City Ballet.
Below
Maria Tallchief and Erik Bruhn for the New York City Ballet.

Index

Numbers in *italics* refer to illustrations

The Chinese Dance (NYCB).

Margot Fonteyn, 1937.

Jillanna with Snowflakes (NYCB).

In some cases we have not been able to credit individual photographers and have therefore credited the appropriate ballet company.

U.S. Edition
Library of Congress Cataloging in Publication Data
Anderson, Jack, 1935–
    The nutcracker ballet.
    1. Chaikovskii, Petr Il'ich, 1840–1893. The
nutcracker. 2. The nutcracker (Ballet) I. Title.
ML410.C4A6   782.9'5'0924   79–1307
ISBN 0-8317-6486-4

Acknowledgements

The publisher would like to thank Adam and Charles Black Publishers for their kind permission to reproduce the original scenario from The Nutcracker published in 1960, Dance Magazine to reprint extracts from the article on The Nutcracker by Jack Anderson published in December 1966, and Les Ballets Trockadero de Monte Carlo to reproduce their program notes to The Nutcracker Ballet. The publisher would also like to thank Derrick E Witty, the London Festival Ballet and the Royal Ballet Press Office for their kind assistance in the compilation of pictures for this book.

Picture Credits

Ballet West 23 (bottom), 36/37, 44 (bottom), 57, 68/69, 113, 173 (both), 174 (bottom), 184 (left), 204 (both), 205 (top).
The Boston Ballet 52/53, 166 (top), 188/189.
The Cincinnati Ballet Company 9 (bottom), 11 (top), 43 (top), 44 (top), 45, 46/47 (both), 48, 132, 133 (both), 169 (both), 174 (top).
Selma Jeanne Cohen 17.
Anthony Crickmay front jacket, jacket flap, back jacket, title page, contents page, 6/7, 14/15, 42/43, 56, 76/77, 100 (bottom), 114/115, 119 (same as front jacket), 144/145, 146, 148/149, 158/159, 170/171, 172, 176 (bottom), 185 (right), 186 (top), 200/201.
Alan Cunliffe 72/73.
Zöe Dominic 177.
Ken Hillier 98/99.
Mike Humphrey 140/141.
Peggy Leder 164/165, 168.
London Festival Ballet 62/63, 95, 99 (bottom left), 147, 160/161, 176 (top), 205 (bottom).
Nigel Luckhurst 152, 186 (bottom).
McBean 181 (bottom).
Minnesota Dance Theater 106/107, 109 (top left), 116/117, 134/135, 137 (both insets), 138/139.
National Association for Regional Ballet 130/131, 189.
Novosti 18/19 (both), 23 (top), 28, 29, 30 (top), 31 (both), 41 (both), 80, 81 (both), 84/85 (both), 86, 87, 88/89 (all three), 210/211.
Radio Times Hulton Picture Library 16 (both), 21, 49 (both), 78, 79, 82, 83 (all three), 94 (top and bottom), 99 (top right), 101, 103, 221.
Houston Rogers 12/13, 102, 208/209.
Royal Ballet Press Office 100 (top), 162.
Royal Winnipeg Ballet 27, 71, 108/109 (bottom), 109 (top right), 128, 129.
Frank Sharman FRPS 99 (bottom right).
Donald Southern 164 (top), 178/179 (all three).
Michael Stannard 70, 187, 191.
Martha Swope 12 (top), 24/25, 30 (bottom), 32, 35, 50/51, 54/55, 58, 61, 64, 65, 66, 67, 74/75, 104/105, 110/111 (both), 112, 122/123, 124, 125, 126/127, 133 (top), 136/137, 142, 143, 150/151 (both), 153, 154/155, 156/157 (all three), 163, 181 (top), 182/183, 184/185, 188 (left), 190, 192/193, 194/195, 196/197 (both), 198/199, 202, 203, 206/207, 212/213, 214/215, 216/217, 218 (both), 219 (both), 220, 222, 224.
Theatre Museum, Victoria and Albert Museum, London 10 (bottom), 60, 72 (left), 90/91 (both), 92, 93 (both), 94 (center), 96 (left), 166/167, 180 (both).
John Vickers 96/97.
Richard Wisdom 8, 9 (top), 118, 120, 175.

Overleaf
Melissa Hayden (NYCB).